CHRISTIANITY
IN ENGLAND

AN HISTORICAL SKETCH

Pearse

BY

C. A. ALINGTON

D.D., Dean of Durham
Honorary Fellow of Trinity College, Oxford

OXFORD UNIVERSITY PRESS

OXFORD UNIVERSITY PRESS
AMEN HOUSE, E.C.4
London Edinburgh Glasgow New York
Toronto Melbourne Capetown Bombay
Calcutta Madras
HUMPHREY MILFORD
PUBLISHER TO THE UNIVERSITY

First printed 1942
Reprinted with corrections 1943

PRINTED IN GREAT BRITAIN
BY WESTERN PRINTING SERVICES LTD., BRISTOL

PREFACE

A 'SKETCH' implies selection of what the picture is to contain, and no one can know so well as the author of this 'historical sketch' how difficult the process of selection is. I can only claim that I have tried my best not to misrepresent those with whom my sympathy is imperfect. I need hardly say that the inevitable omission of any reference to the activities of the Roman Catholic Church since the Reformation must not be taken to imply any doubt of their essential Christianity.

I should like to express my gratitude to the Bishop who has corrected my history, to the two Head Masters who, besides encouraging me to attempt the task, have endeavoured to modify the rigour of my orthodoxy and to remove the obscurities of my style, and to my publishers, who have saved me from many blunders, large and small.

I hope that those which remain will not obscure the purpose of the book, which is to suggest that in an application of Christian principles—and, where necessary, a return to them —lies the only real hope for the future of the country.

C. A. A.

CONTENTS

INTRODUCTION

THE object of this book is to show the influence which Christianity has had in the last two thousand years. It does not assume that those who use it would all call themselves Christians, though naturally the writer hopes that they do so, or will do so: but in any case there is no denying how great its effect has been on the world, and every intelligent person must wish to know what it has tried to do and how far it has succeeded.

Broadly speaking, the Christian Church exists to try to convince mankind that Jesus Christ was right when He said that the best name that we could give to God was that of Love— that He was the Father of all mankind and that all men were therefore brothers. Christians maintain that He proclaimed these truths with authority because He was Himself the Son of God, sent by His Father to proclaim them to the world.

That is, of course, what is called a 'doctrinal' question, but Christ Himself said, 'If any man will do his will, he shall know of the doctrine (or teaching) whether it be of God', so that it is right to begin at what we may call the practical end, though to suppose that we can do without doctrine is a ridiculous mistake. The test of any doctrine is whether it works in practice.

This book suggests that whenever the Christian Church has been true to its Master's teaching, it has, in fact, 'worked'. It is very far from suggesting that it has always been true to that teaching, and gives some reasons why it has failed, but any one who thinks for a moment will see that it is a tremendous task to teach men to live like brothers, and will be quite as much surprised at its success as at its failures.

Comparatively little is said of the failures in this book, not because they have not been real and scandalous, but because there is no sort of reason why people should not fail who only call themselves Christians and do not really try to live on Christian principles.

Again, very little has been said of the divisions among Christians, or of the reasons for them: the writer naturally believes that on the main points the Church of England is in the right, but neither he nor the Church to which he belongs maintains that it has always been either wise or charitable, and both he and it believe that the points on which Christians are agreed are infinitely more important than those on which they differ. His object is to show by a few examples through the centuries what Christianity has done in the face of enormous difficulties, and to suggest thereby what it can do in the present day.

I

SMALL BEGINNINGS—TO A.D. 325

We must begin by a short sketch of the origins of the Christian religion. It might truly be said that Christianity started with almost every possible disadvantage. It began in a small out-of-the-way province: it was preached originally by Jews, whom most other nations disliked for keeping so closely to themselves, as they do still. (They tried to keep Christianity to themselves and to make every Christian accept Jewish customs and it was only after a hard fight that they gave in on this point.)

Then, again, the Founder of Christianity had been put to a shameful death, and though His followers said that He had risen again and that they had seen Him and spoken with Him, the first fact was much easier to believe than the second. And His followers, as we see from the Gospels, had not always by any means understood what He said: they had, for about thirty years, no written records to help them, and could only preach what they had heard themselves or been told by others. It was a tremendous undertaking for people like this to set out to convert the world. But they *did* 'convert' the world, or at least the Roman world, in less than three hundred years: how was it done?

Our first few pictures will try to suggest the answer.

Let us begin with St. Paul's visit to Athens. This was not of course the first time that Christianity had been preached in Europe; that had come after the dramatic moment when St. Paul in a vision or a dream saw 'a man of Macedonia' saying 'Come over and help us'; he took it as a message from God and obeyed. But Athens was very different from Macedonia: it was intellectually the capital of the ancient world: the Athenians, as every one agreed, were the cleverest of people, and they were quite conscious of it themselves: they loved arguments of all kinds and not least arguments about religion.

Their city was, as it still is, one of the most beautiful places in the world, containing perhaps the finest buildings ever made by man, looking out over a bright blue sea: they were very proud of this and of their climate, which (they said) helped them to be so quick-witted, so unlike the stupid Boeotians a few miles away.

So much for the scene and the audience: now for the speaker. St. Paul was not an impressive figure: he says himself that his enemies called his 'bodily presence weak'. The only early account we have of his appearance speaks of him as small, with meeting eyebrows, with a rather large nose, bald-headed, and bowlegged. Nor was he a great orator: some said his 'natural speech was contemptible'. But he had something he meant to say, and he wanted to say it in a way which the Athenians would appreciate: so he began with a compliment, telling them that he saw, from all the temples in the city, that they were a people interested in religion.[1]

In a sense this was true; the city was full of beautiful temples and glorious statues, and there were many great religious ceremonies, but it is doubtful whether many of the intelligent Athenians really believed in their gods, many of the stories about whom were very discreditable. In any case they could not help seeing that it was ridiculous to have gods quarrelling and competing with one another, and it was not much comfort to believe that behind them all was a blind and impersonal fate which really settled everything.

St. Paul had seen an altar inscribed 'To God unknown', and he took that as his text for suggesting that they were still looking for a god in whom they could really believe. If there was such a god, he could not be thought to live in any temple, however splendid, and no statue, however fine, could really represent him: such a god must be the 'Lord of heaven and earth' and the creator of all mankind. It followed from that that all men were his children and brothers of one another— an idea which had occurred to one of their own poets.

So far there was nothing to shock them, but when he went on to say that Jesus Christ was the Son of God, that He had been raised from the dead and would come one day to judge the world, we cannot be surprised that they were both shocked

---

[1] The word translated 'superstitious', Acts xvii. 22, clearly means this: he would never have begun by being rude.

and indignant.[1] They called him a 'babbler', and though a few were ready to hear more, and still fewer believed what they heard, he did not have any great success in Athens, and seems not to have been satisfied that he had put his case as well as he should.

But, whether it was a success or not, his speech had brought out some of the most important things in Christianity, and specially important for Athenians to hear. If all men were 'children of God' the Athenians had no right to regard themselves as a superior race of beings, as they certainly did. It is a common temptation, to which the Germans have yielded now, and it is impossible to say that the British have not suffered from it also. To despise a man for being of a different race, or colour, from yourself is a definitely unChristian thing.

It is still more obvious that to make other men your slaves is wrong, and the Athenian society was based on slave labour: many of their slaves were not ill-treated (though those who worked in the mines were), but the whole principle was wrong. Christ never preached about slavery, and St. Paul never went further than saying that a Christian master must treat his slave as his equal in God's sight: it took eighteen hundred years before Christians agreed that slavery was a disgrace, and there is nothing more glorious in the history of this country than the part it played in abolishing it.[2] There is no more Christian act in the history of nations.

Again if all mankind are equal in God's sight, what about women? In Athens the wife was kept very much in the background—more so, for instance, than at Rome—but Christianity from the first put men and women on an equality. Christ never preached about it but He shocked His disciples by treating women (even bad women) with consideration, and after many centuries this teaching has borne fruit as another of the slow-won victories of Christianity.[3]

[1] It is interesting to notice that they seem to have thought when he preached of 'the resurrection' that he was preaching a new goddess, for the Greek word *anastasis* is rather like a proper name.

[2] See page 140.

[3] St. Paul was not always quite consistent on this point, but it should never be forgotten that it was he who said that in God's sight there was no difference between male and female, just as there was no difference between Jew and Greek or between slave and freeman.

This is, of course, only a specimen of St. Paul's preaching, and perhaps not the most successful one: you will find plenty of other examples in Acts and in his letters, and will see that though he changed his style to suit his hearers or readers, he always gave much the same message, and always urged the same virtues.[1] (Take for example, Eph. iv. 25–end.) It is not to be supposed that the Christians to whom he preached all practised these virtues—indeed we know that they did not, nor have all Christians practised them ever since: but enough of them did so to make a real impression on the heathen world, as we shall see later on.

It is worth noticing that many of St. Paul's converts came from the poorer and less educated classes: as he says, there were 'not many wise, not many learned' among them, and the same is true of the converts in India, for instance, to-day. It is easy to sneer at this result, but as Christianity is based on the Fatherhood of God and the brotherhood of man it is natural that it should appeal most directly to those who had been forgotten and neglected by other religions. As St. Paul's letters show, he was very ready to argue with the learned, but he taught that the great truths of Christianity are so simple that no great learning is needed to appreciate them.

It is interesting to remember that, as has been said, the early Christian preachers had none of our written documents on which to rely: the earliest Gospels, as we have them, did not appear till A.D. 60, though some of the writings on which they were based may have appeared some ten years earlier. St. Paul's Epistles were no doubt sent round from church to church, but there cannot have been many copies of them, and they do not attempt to give a full account of the faith, but only to deal with particular questions.

Preaching is not a very dramatic subject (though it is pleasant to recall the picture of St. John, when he was too old and feeble to preach, contenting himself with the short sermon 'Little children, love one another'). But it is important to remember that, with all its difficulties, the work was done, and that in the course of two or three centuries the civilized

[1] Every one ought to know by heart his great hymn in praise of Love, 1 Cor. xiii.

world did come to have some definite idea what Christianity meant. This idea probably came as much from the lives of Christians as from their sermons, and in our next picture we shall give one of the ways in which they showed their character.

During most of the first three centuries Christians were liable to persecution. At first the trouble came mainly from Jews who hated them, or from citizens like the worshippers of Diana at Ephesus, whose business they seemed likely to damage. In the early days the Roman governors (like Gallio at Corinth) could be trusted to see fair play, but before long some Roman emperors like Nero became very hostile: he took advantage of the unpopularity of the Jews, with whom Christians were at first confused, and put on them the blame for the fire of Rome, burning many of them to death.

Gradually it became established that Christians (who would not burn incense to the Emperor as a god) were enemies to the State, and might be persecuted at any time. Good emperors and good governors did not put the law into force, and did not go out of their way to seek them out and punish them, but a bad or a legally minded emperor might change this policy,[1] and if there was a local outcry it might sometimes be difficult even for a good governor to protect them, for they were the wrong side of the law.

Two or three illustrations will show the kind of thing which might happen.

Early in the second century (A.D. 110) IGNATIUS, bishop of Antioch, was arrested and taken to Rome to be thrown to the wild beasts. We know a good deal about him, because we have the letters which he wrote on his journey to Rome. He calls Ephesus 'a highway of those on their way to be killed for God's sake', so we must suppose that this form of punishment was fairly common.

He was chained to ten soldiers—he called them 'ten leopards who get worse the better one treats them'. So far from being afraid, he was anxious to get to Rome and face the wild beasts: he begs the Romans in his letter to them not to

---

[1] So might a good emperor if he was a conservative by nature and wished to see old customs maintained.

try to save him. 'I am in love with death' he says, and again, 'I am God's corn, and I shall be ground by the teeth of the wild beasts to be made pure bread for Christ.' He thanks God that he has been counted worthy to win honour for Him.

This seems to us a little exaggerated, and indeed the Church did not approve of people who courted martyrdom: it was one thing to die if you must, but quite another to thrust yourself into danger without cause until the question arose of denying your faith.

Here is the story of another bishop, put to death a little later. POLYCARP of Smyrna was an old man: he had been a disciple of St. John, so that he was a close link with Gospel times. There was a violent persecution in Smyrna at the time of the great games in honour of the emperor: many Christians refused to sacrifice to him and were tortured and put to death: then the crowd raised the cry, 'Away with the atheists! Look for Polycarp!' His friends persuaded him, much against his will, to leave the town and go to a farm close by: there he stayed, spending his time in prayer 'for all men and for all the Churches in the world', and one night as he prayed he seemed in a vision to see the pillow at his head on fire: he turned and said to his companions 'I must needs be burnt alive'. Soon after, his hiding place was betrayed by a child, and late one evening the soldiers came to take him. He could have escaped, but refused to fly, saying 'God's will be done'.

He came down to meet the soldiers, and talked to them, giving orders that they should be given meat and drink: his only request was that he might have time to say his prayers: when they gave him leave he stood and prayed for two hours 'making mention of all with whom he had ever had to do, great and small, obscure and famous alike, and praying for the whole Catholic Church throughout the whole world', while those who heard him listened with wonder, and many of the soldiers were sorry they had come to lay hands on so fine an old man.

They brought him to the city, and one of the officials and his father tried to persuade him to change his mind, saying, 'What is the harm in saying "Caesar is Lord" and sacrificing and saving your life?' At first he gave them no answer, but at last he said, 'I cannot do what you advise.' Then they turned to abuse, and Polycarp was rudely hustled into the stadium 'where there was such a tumult that no one could hear a word.' But as Polycarp entered there were some who thought they heard a voice which said, 'Be strong, Polycarp, and play the man.'

The noise grew greater till the proconsul began to question him, and to urge him to have respect for his grey hairs. 'Take an oath', he said, '"by the fortune of Caesar", repent, and say "Away with the atheists".' This last order Polycarp could obey: he looked at the crowd in the stadium, and pointing to them with his finger said sadly enough, 'Yes, away with the atheists!'

The proconsul persevered and said, 'Only take the oath, and I will let you go free. Curse Christ.' Then Polycarp made his famous answer, 'Eighty and six years have I served Him, and in nothing has He done me wrong: how can I blaspheme against my King, who saved me?' Then he added, 'If you think I can swear by the fortune of Caesar, and if you pretend not to know who I am, I tell you plainly, I am a Christian. If you wish to learn what Christianity is, give me a day and listen to what I will tell you.'

'Try to persuade the crowd', said the proconsul. 'They have no right to an answer from me', answered Polycarp. 'You are a governor, and we Christians are taught to respect the powers ordained by God: I will speak to you, not to them.' 'I can throw you to the wild beasts', said the governor, 'or to the fire unless you repent.'

But Polycarp only answered, 'To repent cannot mean to change from what is better to what is worse. The fire with which you threaten me burns but for a moment, but there is a fire of judgement to come which burns for ever. Do what you will.'

The proconsul was amazed, and sent his herald to proclaim three times in the stadium. 'Polycarp has confessed that he is a Christian.' The whole mob roared out, 'This is the teacher of Asia! the father of the Christians! the destroyer of our gods! he teaches men not to worship them or do sacrifice!' They shouted that the Asiarch (who presided over the Jews) should throw Polycarp to the lions, but he refused, saying the games were over, so they all cried that he must be burnt.

So they seized wood from the shops and brought faggots and made a pyre: Polycarp made no resistance, but stripped himself to make ready: only when they would have nailed him to the post did he make a protest, saying, 'Let me be: for He who has given me strength to face the fire will give me strength to stand on the pyre unshrinking, without the help of nails.' So they were content only to bind him to the post.

Polycarp looked up to heaven and said: 'O Lord God Almighty, Father of Thy beloved and blessed son, Jesus Christ, through Whom we have received the full knowledge of Thee . . . I bless Thee that Thou hast thought me worthy of this day and hour. . . . May I be received this day among Thy martyrs as an acceptable sacrifice, O God, Who art true and canst not lie. For this and for all things I praise and bless and glorify Thee, through Thy beloved son, our eternal and heavenly high priest, Jesus Christ, through Whom be glory to Thee with Him and the Holy Spirit now and for ever, Amen.'

Then the fire was kindled, and so Polycarp died.

We have told this story at length because of its beauty. There were many similar scenes all over the Roman empire, but it was only in the third century that two emperors, Decius and Diocletian, definitely attempted to stamp out Christianity: one of them tried to do it by seizing and burning their sacred books and the other by killing their ministers and officials.

These persecutions, which, though they did not last very long, were very violent and extended everywhere, gave rise to many difficulties later on. As was to be expected, many so-called Christians gave way sooner than be killed. Sometimes they handed over their bibles and were called *traditores* (from which comes our word traitor): sometimes they consented to sacrifice, or got a certificate to say they had done so, whether it was true or not. They were called *libellatici*, certificate men. When the persecution was over these men wanted to be received back into the Church, and at once difficulties began:

some people thought they should be forgiven at once, others that they should never be forgiven at all. Then there was another question: if your priest had been a *traditor* or a *libellaticus*, was it worse for him than for a layman? could he be regarded as a true priest at all?

People felt so strongly on both sides, especially in Africa, where they were very hot-tempered, that there grew up a schism (or division) in the Church which took a long time to heal, for those who took the strict view could have no dealings with the others. You will see that there is much to be said on both sides, for it is difficult to respect a man who is only a Christian as long as there is no danger in being one, and at the same time Christians know that they ought to forgive those who have done wrong if they repent. Then the question arises, Do they really repent? or are they only pretending to be sorry?

It would be interesting to try to make up your mind on which side you would have been, though it is to be hoped that whichever view you took you would not have felt it necessary to break off all dealings with those who disagreed with you.

II

SUCCESS AND ITS RESULTS—TO A.D. 597

However it came about, whether by their preaching, or by their lives (and deaths), the Christians did succeed in converting the Empire, and by about A.D. 325 Christianity was recognized as its religion.

Of course, many people accepted Christianity simply because the Emperor Constantine had done so. This imaginary dialogue will give some idea of how things looked about that time to two ordinary Romans, one a strong conservative, and one more open-minded. It need hardly be said that it attempts only to reproduce their ideas and not their actual words.

Marcus. You mark my words—that emperor of yours is going to turn Christian!

Caius. I don't know why you call Constantine *my* emperor, just because he was born at York, and I served some time in Britain! He's your emperor just as much as mine. But why shouldn't he turn Christian if he wants to?

Marcus. They're a cowardly, disloyal lot. They don't approve of fighting, and they won't sacrifice to the emperor: I've no use for them!

Caius. I'm not a Christian myself, but I don't think it's fair to say they don't make good soldiers—I've met plenty of them in the army—and if their religion won't let them do sacrifice it doesn't prove they aren't loyal. Why, any number of Constantine's troops are Christians!

Marcus. I know, I know! Things have got very slack since that edict of toleration:[1] I always said it was a mistake to let every one be free to worship as he liked.

Caius. That wasn't any special favour to the Christians— it simply gave liberty to all, and I can't see why the Christian shouldn't be as free as any one else.

Marcus. But Constantine's gone much further than that. Look at that statue of him put up in Rome[2]—they said that staff in his hand wasn't a cross, but I know it was! If it wasn't, what was the point of the inscription about 'this saving sign'?

Caius. Well, he says he saw a sign of the Cross in the sky.

Marcus. So he says!

Caius. They say the soldiers saw it too and an inscription under it, 'In this sign thou shalt conquer'. Whether that's true or not, things have gone very well with him ever since, and one can't blame him for believing in it.

Marcus. But does he really believe in it? He told a lot of bishops that 'no one could see into the secrets of his bosom': you mark my words, Constantine's no fool: it's all a matter of politics with him.

Caius. Well, even supposing it is, where's the harm in it? If he thinks the Christians are strong enough why shouldn't

[1] Edict of Milan, A.D. 313.
[2] In A.D. 312.

he take their side as a matter of politics? What would you have him do?

Marcus. Do? Why, what Diocletian began doing! Wipe the brutes out, kill their priests, and destroy their temples!—instead of which we have these edicts restoring all their property, churches being built everywhere, and the emperor addressing parties of Christian 'bishops' (as they call them) almost as if he were of them already! Then take all that business about Sunday! I didn't see any harm in his telling people to 'rest on the venerable day of the sun': I quite see it's a good plan to give people a day's rest: but now I'm told it's the day the Christians keep holy—they've got some story about it being the day when Christ rose from the dead, if you please! And I'm told that Constantine carries a tent church with him and has services on that day, and even lets the legions have tent churches too. I don't know what'll become of discipline in the army, I'm sure.

Caius. I can't say I think persecution was a great success: if people really believe anything, persecution only makes them more determined: look at those forty soldiers at Sebaste the other day!

Marcus. I never heard of them—what did they do?

Caius. I can't promise it's true, but this is the story I heard. There were forty soldiers who wouldn't sacrifice, so they stripped them naked and took them out on a cold winter's night, offering a hot bath to any one who'd give in.

Marcus. That's the way to treat the obstinate brutes! How many stuck it out?

Caius. Thirty-nine: but the point is that, when one of them gave in, the guard was so impressed with the courage of the rest that he took his place, so there were forty martyrs after all. Mind you, I can't swear it's a true story, but that's the kind of thing that does happen: they've got a saying, 'The blood of martyrs is the seed of the Church', and you can't deny there's a lot of truth in it.

Marcus. We shall soon have you turning Christian yourself at this rate!

Caius. No, I don't know enough about their special

beliefs. All I say is that I can't help being struck by their courage: they don't seem to mind what happens to them.

Marcus. There's nothing new about that! our philosophers have been saying for years that the wise man doesn't mind what happens to him.

Caius. Yes, but these people aren't wise men: they're just ordinary people and they seem much more cheerful about it than your philosophers, who always strike me as a gloomy lot. My wife has seen a good deal of them and she tells me . . .

Marcus. Oh come, you surely can't think it's a thing for women to decide!

Caius [*laughing*]. My dear Marcus, I'm ashamed of you! Fancy a good conservative thinking little of Roman matrons! I thought you were so proud of them! Anyhow, according to my wife, the Christians think women as important as men: their idea seems to be that every one is equal in the sight of God.

Marcus. You'll be telling me next that my slave's as good a man as I am! If they once get that idea in their heads, we're in for a revolution, and it'll all be the emperor's fault.

Caius. I agree it's a bit startling, but it so happens one of my slaves is a Christian, and I can't say I've noticed any change in him: he does his work a bit better, that's all. I asked him about it and he said they were told to honour their masters and do what they were told. He's an intelligent fellow, and I was interested in his ideas. He said 'I'm your slave, sir, but in the sight of God I'm a free man, and, if you don't mind my saying so, that's the thing that matters most to me.'

Marcus. Well, I'm too old-fashioned for all these new ideas, and I don't like to see the emperor taking them up. When I was a boy, I remember people saying, 'If the emperor became a Christian', as a sort of absurdity, just as one might say 'if pigs were to fly'—and now it looks as if we were going all to be turned into Christians by Constantine, whether we like it or not!

Caius [*smiling*]. I don't imagine there'll be any compulsion about it, anyhow! But if the emperor *does* become a Christian it's sure to become fashionable. Don't tell me you're so attached to worshipping the emperor that it'd shock your conscience!

Marcus. My conscience doesn't come into it: but I don't like changes at my age. Anything for a quiet life is my motto!

Caius. Poor old Marcus! If that's all you want, I shouldn't be surprised if we see you turning Christian after all! I can't say I think you'll be a very good one, but that's not my business. I only hope the Christians will like you when they get you!

Marcus's fears were fulfilled: Constantine did declare himself a Christian, and presided at Christian conferences. Caius was right too, for Marcus, and many like him, did become Christians in name. To 'convert' the Roman Empire was a very great achievement in so short a time, but all the wisest Christians knew that the conversion was only skin deep, and that there was great danger in Christianity becoming fashionable and powerful. But there were some definite practical results: a Christian lady founded the first charity hospital at Rome in the fourth century—and Christian hospitals spread rapidly: the sick and poor were better cared for, and the condition of slaves improved; it became regarded as a virtuous act to give them their freedom: suicide, which had been regarded as a glorious act, came to be considered a crime. Here is one story which shows how changes came about.

Just after A.D. 400 the Emperor Honorius came to Rome, and gladiatorial games were held in his honour. Just as the fight was beginning, an Eastern monk, called Telemachus, sprang into the arena and tried to separate the combatants. The spectators were furious and pelted him to death, but that was the end of gladiatorial games in Rome, and public opinion was well content when Honorius by an edict abolished them for ever.

Only about a century passed after the empire had become Christian when it was attacked, and much of it conquered, by barbarian tribes—the Visigoths, the Huns, the Vandals, the Ostrogoths, the Lombards, the Franks—these are only some of the names, and some of them, as you will see, can still be seen on the map of Europe—in France, in Lombardy, and in Andalusia (southern Spain). The Church had two tasks, to maintain civilization when the Roman government had to withdraw, and to convert these barbarian invaders to Christianity. These were very hard tasks for so young a Church, and it is more surprising that they were accomplished at all than that they were not done perfectly.

But before we consider them let us look at one picture which shows Church influence at its best.

There was at the end of the fourth century a great and, on the whole, a good emperor, Theodosius. In the year A.D. 390 he heard of a disgraceful outbreak in Salonica: a charioteer who was to have performed in the games was imprisoned by the governor for a serious crime: the people were furious at losing their sport, and murdered the governor and some of his officers. The emperor was naturally indignant and proposed to punish the whole city. AMBROSE, bishop of Milan, and some other bishops, interceded with him—it was regarded as part of a bishop's duty to plead for mercy—and he promised to spare the city. But other advisers persuaded him to change his mind and orders were sent for a general massacre, and though we are told that he repented and sent further orders, they came too late, and seven thousand people were put to death without the slightest form of trial.

Ambrose wrote a letter of protest, and warned the emperor that if he came to a Christian service he could not receive him. Theodosius took no notice and presented himself: Ambrose refused him permission to enter the church unless he was prepared to do penance for his sin. For eight months he stayed away, and did not venture to present himself even at Christmas, but after that he visited Ambrose and asked on what terms he could be readmitted. Ambrose told him that he must make a decree that no capital sentence should be executed until after an interval of thirty days, so as to give time for proper consideration. The emperor agreed: he took off his imperial robes, prostrated himself on the pavement and 'with tears intreated pardon'. It was a great triumph for the Christian principle of mercy.

It is interesting to remember that Ambrose was the first famous writer of Christian hymns: you will find some of them translated in our hymn books. The earliest hymns had no rhyme (which neither the Greeks nor the Romans had used) but naturally it soon crept in.

Ambrose died before the barbarian troubles had begun: our next picture, some thirty years later, shows them at their height. AUGUSTINE, bishop of Hippo in northern Africa, lies dying while the barbarian Vandals besiege the city: the fact that the name 'vandal' has survived shows the kind of reputation which they had won. The siege had lasted for two months, and he saw that the end was coming. He had urged his brother bishops not to desert their people, but he knew what their fate would be: he could only pray that 'God would either deliver Hippo or would strengthen His servants to bear His will.' Hippo was not delivered: Augustine died (A.D. 430) and the whole of northern Africa, which had once been a great stronghold of the Church, fell into the hands of the barbarians. It is hard to believe that it was once so populous a country that there were more than five hundred bishops, though it must be admitted that owing to the dispute about 'traitors' (see p. 14), half of them were out of communion with the rest.

St. Augustine was a great writer as well as a great man. He has written an account of his life in his *Confessions*, where he tells the story of his conversion. He had led a very careless life as a young man in Rome, but one day, as he sat in the garden, he seemed to hear a voice saying, 'Take up the book and read'. He picked up a New Testament which lay by his side (for he was interested in Christianity though not yet a Christian), and opened it at random: the verse on which he opened (Rom. xiii. 13) was a warning to abandon sin and to follow Christ. From that moment he was converted, finding, as he says himself, that 'God has made us for Himself, and our heart is restless till it find rest in Him.'

His other great book, the *City of God*, was written when he heard that Rome had been taken by the barbarians (A.D. 410): to him, and to every one else in the empire, this seemed like the end of the world, so he wrote a book in which he draws a contrast between the city of God in heaven, which can never be taken, and the capital of an earthly empire, and tried to show how the kingdom of God could be realized on earth. He was a Roman, and the Romans were all legal-minded— their laws were the greatest thing they gave to the world—and perhaps he was too much inclined to think of God as a judge, and also to think of the Church too much as a great earthly society. His authority was so great for many centuries that he was made responsible for much of which he would have disapproved. Some people have thought that it was his fault that in the Middle Ages the Church, under its great popes, tried to establish its power by very worldly means, but this would certainly have shocked him, though he would have liked the idea that the head of the Church was greater than any earthly king.

One difficulty in the way of the conversion of the barbarians was that the Church at this time was much divided by what is called the Arian heresy.

Very roughly speaking, Arius thought that though Christ was a son of God, he could not be *the* son of God, or equal to Him, for that would mean that there were two Gods, and that a son could be equal to his father. It followed that He could not perfectly explain the will of God, who remained unknowable.[1]

To this the Christian answer is that if we cannot know what God is like religion is impossible: that when we say Christ is the Son of God we mean that God is Christlike, and that we can trust Christ to express His will. That is the reason why we claim to know that God is Love. The final truth about God cannot be put into words, and Arius was wrong in trying to be so logical. Even if you try only to describe a great piece of music, or a beautiful view, in words, you will find that they break down, and it is not surprising that they break down when you try to describe the nature of God.

But Arius and his followers were quite honest and very zealous, and though the Church decided against them, they remained numerous and powerful, and were very active

[1] Mr. H. G. Wells has much the same idea when he calls the Creator the 'Veiled Being' of whom one can really know nothing: he is a kind of fate behind everything. But no one can worship a blind fate or a god who is not almighty.

missionaries, so that when the time came to try to convert the barbarians many of them were converted by these heretical Arians.[1]

This was a great pity, for tribes converted by the Arians never could get on with the 'orthodox' Christians whom they conquered, and in some countries, like Spain, it took many centuries before the country was really united.

It was very lucky for the Franks that their king, Clovis, (from whom the name Louis comes) was converted by an 'orthodox' missionary: this gave the Franks a start which they never lost, and France was the first of the new 'barbarian' kingdoms to become a really strong power.

Clovis cannot be called a good specimen of a Christian convert: he was a bloodthirsty ruffian, and probably neither his conversion nor that of his followers was very real. But he said a fine thing when he heard of the story of the crucifixion: he gripped his sword and cried out, 'Why was I not there with my Franks?'

Sometimes the conversion was accomplished by missionaries, but perhaps more was done by the example of the bishops who stayed at their posts when the Roman government and its troops disappeared. They kept civilization going, and the barbarians, who could see that this meant a better life than any they had known, came gradually to accept it and the Christianity which lay behind it.

It is time to say something of the monks, who played a great part in the life of Europe for a thousand years. The word 'monk' means one who lives alone, and the first monks were men who retired into the deserts of Egypt and so got the name 'hermits', or dwellers in the desert. The most famous of these was St. Antony (A.D. 251–356), who retired into the desert at the age of twenty and lived what was in the main a solitary life for more than eighty years. His belief was that it was impossible to live a perfect life in the world, and that as Christ had told His followers to be 'perfect', the only thing to do was to leave it altogether and so avoid temptation.

Many people followed his example, and lived lives of very

---

[1] A heretic is a man who chooses his own belief, in preference to that accepted by the Church.

great hardship, eating hardly anything and spending their time in prayer and meditation. They were often men of beautiful character, and some charming stories are told about them, but most Christians will feel that the sort of perfection at which they aimed is not that which Christ meant.

When the barbarian invasions threw the whole Roman world into confusion the desire to leave it became more common, and a great man, St. BENEDICT (A.D. 480–543), took advantage of this feeling to found a monastery which became the pattern for all others. The hermits by this time had been inclined to gather into groups, and Benedict's monastery was not a place for solitary retirement, but one where people who wished to live 'unspotted by the world' could do so in company.

Another great difference between the monks and the hermits was that the monks were bidden not only to pray, but to work for the common good, for Benedict's motto was 'Work is Prayer' (*Laborare est orare*). At first this work naturally took the form of gardening and agriculture, but it gradually developed into study and teaching, and for a long time the monastery was the best, if not the only, school in Christendom, and also the chief dispenser of charity.

Later on, the monks were encouraged to copy and to illuminate manuscripts, and most of the literature of Greece and Rome which we have was saved by them: thus they became the headquarters of learning and of art—though it is doubtful whether Benedict would have approved of this development.

But their main duty was that of prayer: they had services seven times a day, beginning at 6 o'clock in the morning and ending at midnight.

It is easy to see how beautiful and how peaceful their life must have been at its best: in the monastery there was a peace which certainly could not be found in the world in the fifth century and for many centuries after it. The life of a good monk in a good monastery is one of the most attractive we can imagine. He has no worldly cares: he lives among people who all share his faith and his ideals. His life is ordered for him, but he is free to work at whatever task suits him best:

to grow fruit or flowers: to copy manuscripts and paint them: to teach the young: to distribute help to the poor: to use any gifts he may have for the good of the brethren. (You will find a delightful picture of a good monastery in Carlyle's *Past and Present*.) But there were some great dangers about it, and the 'monastic' movement did great harm as well as great good.

One obvious danger was that the monastery would attract idle people who only wanted a quiet life, and were thinking of themselves much more than of the service of God. It is easy to see that if many such men were admitted (and it was hard to keep them out) the standard of the whole society would soon fall.

Again, men went into monasteries to avoid the temptation of the world, and surrendered all their private property to avoid the temptation to care for riches. But the society, or the monastery, was allowed to hold property, and gradually acquired a great deal, so that the temptation came back in another form. Monasteries became very rich, and also great landowners. Sometimes they spent their money well, and we owe to them many of our greatest churches; on the whole they were good landlords, though not always, and if their abbots and priors were the wrong sort of men it was easy to spend money, given for the service of God and the relief of the poor, on selfish display and even luxury. It was this fault, to be found in a great many monasteries though not in all, which was to ruin them in the end.

Also, it was a serious disaster to the Church that people came to regard the life of a monk as the true Christian life, or indeed the only 'religious' life, and it is to be feared that the monks themselves rather encouraged this idea. The result was that the ordinary life of a Christian family was regarded as an inferior state, and Europe lost the service of many men who might have borne witness to Christianity in its everyday affairs. It is very desirable that there should be some who give their time to praying for those who do not pray for themselves, but from a wider point of view retirement into a monastery might mean to despair of the world, and might encourage the idea that it could not be made a more Christian place. And it is one of the great glories of Christianity that it does not despair of the ordinary man.[1]

Another great change which came over Christendom was the growth of the power of the bishop of Rome (who was first called 'pope' about the year A.D. 400). The bishops of Rome had always been regarded with special respect, partly because Rome was the capital, and partly because it was believed (on very doubtful authority) that St. Peter was its first bishop.

Gradually the popes came to claim authority over the whole Church, though this was never universally accepted: the Eastern Church never accepted it, and the Christian Churches in Russia, Greece, and the Balkans do not accept it to-day. But the rest of Christendom did accept it, till the Reformation, when much of Europe, including England, refused to acknowledge it any longer. But for nearly 1,000 years the pope was accepted in all western Europe as the head of the Church. Sometimes the claims were carried very far and the pope claimed to be the direct representative of God on earth, with authority to depose kings and to say how kingdoms should be governed. Sometimes this power was used wisely by great and good men: sometimes it was used only for the benefit of the Church of Rome, which became a state competing with other kingdoms. It was this misuse of power, in the hands of men who were very poor examples of Christianity, which led to the Reformation, but even those who think the papal claims were based on bad history and a wrong interpretation of the Gospel, must realize how important the services of great popes were to Christianity and to civilization. In the lawless centuries of what are called the Dark Ages, it was a very great thing to have some one who could speak on moral questions with an authority which no one questioned and who might be expected to stand up for Christian principles of conduct.

One of the greatest of popes was GREGORY THE GREAT (A.D. 540-604). He was a rich and distinguished Roman citizen (he had been prefect, or mayor, of Rome) who, when he

---

[1] This is the reason why Christianity, though it does not, or should not, 'take sides' in politics, must always sympathize with democracy against tyranny: Christians would say that it is only because all men are children of God that democracy is right in trusting the people.

was thirty-three years old, became a monk, giving up all his property to found monasteries. When he was fifty, he was forced to become pope, much against his will: he was preparing for flight when he was seized and carried off to be made bishop. It was a very anxious time: he says himself that the Roman Church was 'like an old and violently shattered ship admitting the waters on all sides'.

He was a great and good pope who, if he exalted the authority of the bishop of Rome (as he certainly did), always used that authority to secure good discipline and good morals in the Church, and never forgot the cause of the poor.[1] He managed the great church estates well and honestly. Being himself a monk, he naturally favoured the monasteries, but only when they observed their rules strictly. He was much interested in missionary work both among the heretical Arians and the heathen: by us he must always be remembered as the man who sent Augustine[2] on his mission to England, and though the story of his first interest in the English (told by our English historian Bede) is very famous, it must be told again.

Gregory, while still an abbot, passing through the market of Rome, saw some boys exposed for sale as slaves. He was struck by their white skins and golden hair and was filled with pity. He asked from what country they came. 'From Britain', answered the slave owner. 'And are they Christian or heathens?' 'Heathens', was the answer. 'Alas!' said Gregory, 'that such bright faces should be in the power of the prince of darkness. How do you call their nation?' 'They are called Angles.' ''Tis well said!' cried the abbot, 'they have angels' faces: it were meet that they should be fellow-heirs with angels in heaven. What is their native province?' He was told Deira (which practically means Yorkshire): 'They must be rescued', he said '*de ira dei*—from the

---

[1] There is a charming story of his life as abbot of his monastery. He ate little but raw vegetables and fruit, and his mother used to send him some on a silver dish, the only piece of plate which she had kept. One day a shipwrecked sailor came to the monastery and asked for alms: twice he was helped, but when he came the third time it was found there was no more money in the house. Gregory gave him the silver dish, which had come in with fruit that day—and legend tells that the sailor was an angel in disguise.

[2] Not, of course, the Augustine mentioned on p. 21.

wrath of God': and when he heard that their king's name was Aella, he vowed that Alleluia, praise to God, should one day be sung in that distant land.

He never forgot them and would gladly have gone himself to preach in Britain: he actually started, but the pope recalled him, yielding to the outcry of the Romans. When he was himself pope, as we shall see, he took the matter in hand once more.

III

THE CONCERNS OF A POPE

THIS imaginary conversation, between Gregory and his secretary, which may be dated some five years after Gregory became pope, may give some idea of his character, and of the varied duties which a pope had to perform. Most of the words put in his mouth, and all those of importance, are taken from his letters, of which nearly a thousand still survive.

Gregory [*lying on a couch*]. Come in, Probus! We have much writing to do to-day.

Probus. I trust your Holiness is better?

Gregory. The fever has gone, but there is still gout in my hand, and you must write on my behalf.

Probus. I am afraid that my poor Latin will disappoint those who read!

Gregory [*with a smile*]. Those to whom I write know how little I care for cases and moods and tenses and the rules of grammar: it is an indignity to tie up the oracles of God by the laws of a grammarian. What letters have you that need an answer?

Probus. There are many complaints from Sicily, your Holiness. Your agent Peter seems not to have carried out your commands about the estates of the Church there.

Gregory. You must write sharply to Peter: tell him I bade you address him as 'Your Negligence'. Tell him that he must see that the peasants have justice, and that the farmers do not oppress them. I have heard tales of false weights, and of heavy charges for marriages. The Church must be a just landlord. Peter means well, but he is careless: the last horse he sent me was a wretched beast, and he is losing money both on his mares and on his cattle. Tell him that I expect better things. What next?

Probus. There are many questions from monasteries, your Holiness, but to most of them I think I know the answer: there are some which ask that monks should be allowed to keep property of their own, and some which complain that the bishops are claiming authority over them: and there are monks who wish to serve in parish churches.

Gregory. Yes, those questions are easy: the bishop has no right to interfere in the concerns of the monastery: that is for the pope alone. And for the monks the law is clear: a monk may become a curate or a curate become a monk, but no man can be both. And for private property, a man who would hold it has nothing of the heart of a true monk: the rule of Benedict is clear. How can a man despise the world who, even in a monastery, lusts after gold? Are there no harder questions?

Probus. Yes, my Lord: it seems that the emperor is still forbidding soldiers to become monks till their term of service is ended.

Gregory. Ah, that is an old and difficult question: we will leave it for the moment: there is another and a graver matter whereon we must write to the Serene Emperor. What is that other packet of letters by your hand?

Probus. These are letters from bishops, my Lord, through-out the world—from Africa, from the Frankish kingdom, from Egypt and from Spain, all asking for guidance; not all are urgent, but the courier for Spain leaves in two days, if your Paternity has any letters he would send there.

Gregory. That is well thought of: write to my dear brother, Leander of Seville, telling him how I rejoice that God continues to bless his efforts to win the Visigoths to the Catholic faith. Would that I myself might win over our Lombards in Italy from their Arian folly![1]

[1] The Visigoths in Spain and the Lombards in Italy had both been converted by Arian missionaries.

Probus. Surely, my Lord, God will bless your efforts too.

Gregory. So we must pray! Meanwhile there is another cause that we must take in hand. Write to Candidus, who is going to Gaul, and bid him spend some of our revenues there in buying English slaves, that we may train them as missionaries to their own people. England is a fair land, and must not longer be left in darkness.

Probus. Have you other letters for Candidus to take, my Lord?

Gregory. Yes, indeed! I hear that Desiderius, the bishop of Vienne, is reading heathen poets with his pupils: write to him that it is an abominable thing for a bishop to recite verses which are unfit even for a layman to read. The same mouth cannot sing the praises of Jupiter and the praises of Christ. Tell him that I trust the report is false.

And write to the bishop of Marseilles that he must not destroy the pictures in the churches. Pictures are to the unlearned what books are to the learned: it is for him to see that they do not become objects of worship. And there should be a letter too to Brynhilda, the Queen Regent:[1] come, Probus, why do you look so strangely?

Probus [*stammering*]. I have heard, my Lord, that she is a very evil woman.

Gregory. We must not believe all we hear, and we are bidden not to speak evil of dignities. The Church in Gaul is in an evil state: the clergy are freed slaves, and many of the bishops, I fear, are men who care more for money and luxury than for the things of God. If the Queen Regent can bring them to reform their lives, we must not despise her help. But that is a letter which must wai⁺ till I can write it myself. Forget not the old saying, Probus, that more flies are caught by a spoonful of honey than by a whole barrel of vinegar!

Probus [*relieved*]. You said, my lord, that there was a letter which should go to the emperor at Constantinople.

Gregory [*frowning*]. Yes, and that is one which you can write, saying that the gout forbids me to hold a pen. Tell the Serene Emperor that I grieve from my heart that he maintains

---

[1] Brynhilda, Queen Regent of much of Gaul, was a very wicked woman and Gregory has been much blamed for his respectful language to her.

his edict forbidding soldiers to become monks: his army will increase as the army of God shall increase in prayer.

And warn him against the claims of the bishop of Constantinople, whom men call John the Faster. He is styling himself, we hear, Universal Bishop, an unspeakable title, and an insult to the see of St. Peter.[1] Even the bishops of Rome claim no such name: it is a wicked and blasphemous title, a proud and pompous phrase! The bishop of Rome asks only to be known as the slave of the slaves of God. Warn the Serene Emperor that his dignity too is offended by so monstrous a claim. That is enough, Probus: I am tired and must rest.

Probus. Indeed your Holiness is too careless of health: the care of all the churches presses too heavily upon you.

Gregory [*smiling*]. I can face all things, Probus, provided that I save my soul. But tell my little choristers I cannot give them their singing lesson to-day: perhaps they will be glad not to see the pope among them with his whip![2]

One thing more. See that the twelve poor men are duly fed at my table and be sure that my charities suffer not from my illness. Our property is the property of the poor and I its steward. Remember that you cannot help me more than by giving me the opportunity of doing a kindness, for we seek the rewards of heaven rather than the riches of the earth.

IV

THE EARLY DAYS OF THE CHURCH IN ENGLAND —TO A.D. 1066

So far we have been trying to give, in the roughest outline, some idea of the new ideas which Christianity brought into

---

[1] The Patriarch of Constantinople, which was now the capital of the Roman Empire, wished to claim equality with the bishops of Rome (see p. 26). The popes were in a few centuries to claim the title which Gregory regarded as blasphemous.

[2] It has been thought that Gregory invented the Gregorian music which bears his name: this appears to be untrue, though he was much interested in it, and there may be truth in the tradition that he actually taught his choristers.

Europe, and of the way in which those ideas developed. We have seen how the Roman Empire, and the barbarians, were 'converted', and how much and how little that conversion meant: we have seen the monasteries come into existence, the power of the popes growing, and the kind of disputes which divided Christians. We have now to see how Christianity conquered England, which, we must remember, was a very small and insignificant island in those days—so remote that the Romans had spoken of the Britons as 'utterly divided from the whole world'.

In A.D. 596 Pope Gregory bade AUGUSTINE, the prior of one of his monasteries, to undertake a mission to the English. Augustine was not very eager to go, indeed he turned back once on the way ('struck with a sluggish timorousness' Bede says), but Gregory sent him off again next year with letters, among others, to the Queen Regent Brynhilda (see p. 30) asking her to help him on his way.

We must not blame Augustine too much: Britain was a very distant land, and the Anglo-Saxons, the barbarians who had conquered the Britons, had a bad name for cruelty and for hatred of Christianity.

For Christianity had been established in Britain in Roman times. It probably came with the Roman legions or as a result of the commercial dealings between Britain and Rome. At the beginning of the third century Tertullian speaks of 'the districts of the Britons' as being 'subjugated to the Church', and in Wales at any rate it seems to have gained a firm hold. We hear of several British bishops at the Council of Arles in A.D. 314 and of one British martyr, ST. ALBAN, whose story, as told by Bede, is worth recording. Alban, when a pagan, gave shelter to a Christian priest fleeing from persecution: he watched his guest's habits and was struck with his perseverance in prayer 'by day and night'; he asked for instruction and accepted the Christian faith. When soldiers came to arrest the fugitive, Alban met them and surrendered himself. He was taken to the magistrate, who gave him the choice between offering sacrifice and being put to death. He refused to sacrifice, and after being scourged was beheaded in a meadow near the city of Verulamium, which now bears his name.

But when the Roman troops were withdrawn and Saxon pirates invaded the country, everything Roman was swept away and the British Christians retired into Wales and Cornwall. Their religion grew stronger under persecution and danger, but they hated the Saxons too much to have any wish to convert them.

It is impossible to blame them, for the Saxon invaders had behaved with the greatest cruelty to the Britons. We read that they were 'the most ferocious of all enemies', that they made it a point of religion 'to torture their captives rather than put them to ransom', and to sacrifice the tenth part of them to their gods. Britain had been devastated by them, bishops and people alike 'slain in the midst of the streets', and those who survived, 'the miserable remnant', slaughtered in the mountains, or selling themselves as slaves to the invader.[1] To 'convert' the Anglo-Saxons might well seem an impossible task, even if the Britons had been sufficiently forgiving to attempt it.

But one of the Saxon kings, Ethelbert of Kent, had married a Christian princess from Gaul, and it was to his court that Augustine was sent. He landed near Ramsgate, and we have an account of his first meeting with the king. Augustine's party consisted of some forty men and they advanced to meet the king carrying a large silver cross, and a picture of Christ crucified, singing a litany as they came. Ethelbert, afraid of witchcraft, had refused to meet them in a house, but he received them courteously and gave them leave to settle in Canterbury, which has ever since then been the headquarters of the English Church, and there Augustine founded his cathedral.

He converted Ethelbert, who was baptized with many of his people, founded bishoprics at Rochester and London, and sent a mission to Northumbria which converted its king, Edwin, and established a bishopric at York. Bede has a fine story of a council at which Edwin asked his 'wise men' to discuss the new faith. One of them made a beautiful speech in which he compared the life of man to a sparrow which flies for a moment through a lighted hall, and then is lost in

[1] Bright, *Early English Church History*, p. 22; Trevelyan, *History of England*, p. 38.

the stormy darkness outside. No man knows what has gone before or what will come after: if this strange teacher can tell us, let him be heard. The high priest, Coifi, frankly said that the old religion had done nothing for him, and that he was quite ready to see if the Christian god did more for his followers. So Paulinus, the bishop of York, spoke, and after hearing him Coifi cried that he understood the truth and was ready himself to destroy the temples of the old faith: he leapt on his horse, called for arms, and hurled a spear against the temple, bidding his followers to burn it to the ground.

So Northumbria accepted Christianity, but it is not to be supposed that either there or in Kent the people generally quite understood what it meant: in fact, when Edwin was killed in battle by the heathen king of Mercia (the Midlands) Christianity in Northumbria collapsed: the two kings who followed him gave up their faith, and Paulinus fled. It seemed that Christianity would only survive in Kent.

The situation was saved by the Christian Church in Scotland, which itself came from Ireland. Ireland was even more remote from Rome than Britain, and in the fifth and sixth centuries there had grown up a Church there, founded by St. Patrick, very full of the Christian spirit but very unlike that of the rest of the world. A great Irish saint, COLUMBA, settled in the island of Iona on the west coast of Scotland (he died in the year that Augustine came to Kent), and founded an abbey there which had a wonderful influence.[1] At this abbey there was trained a young Northumbrian prince, OSWALD, who was to restore the Christian kingdom of Northumbria.

He gathered together a small army and took up his position near Hexham by the Roman wall: he caused a cross of wood to be made, and held it with his own hands while his men heaped the soil round it. Then he bade his soldiers kneel and 'entreat the true and living God, who knew how just was their cause, to defend them from the proud and fierce enemy'. They charged the enemy, and though his numbers were far greater, the battle of Heavenfield was won (A.D. 634).

Naturally he turned to Iona when he wanted a bishop to

[1] The ruined abbey has recently been restored, and 'the brothers of Iona' are again trying to carry on Columba's work.

help him to restore religion in Northumbria: they sent him a
man who soon returned saying that the people were incapable
of being taught. One of the brethren, named Aidan, suggested that perhaps he had expected too much of very simple
people, and all the company cried out that he himself was the
man to go. So Aidan came to Northumbria, and for eight
years, till Oswald was killed in battle with the heathen, he
and the king established religion in Northumbria, building
churches, founding monasteries, and providing for the education of the people.

AIDAN is the most lovable of all British or English saints,
the only one who can be compared to St. Francis, and his
house at Lindisfarne is as fitting a place of pilgrimage as
Assisi (see p. 62). Here are two stories from Bede which
illustrate his character. The king and the bishop were dining
together in the royal castle of Bamburgh, and 'a silver dish
full of royal dainties' was set before them, when news was
brought that a crowd of poor people was gathered without,
asking alms from the king. Oswald ordered the contents of
the dish to be carried to them and the dish itself to be broken
and divided for their benefit. Aidan seized his right hand,
crying, 'May this hand never decay!' And Bede assures us
that up to his time the prayer had been answered.

After Oswald's death, a king called Oswin reigned in Deira
(or Yorkshire, the southern part of Northumbria). He was
distressed that Aidan had to make long journeys on foot
through his enormous diocese, and gave him a 'horse fit for a
king'. Aidan gratefully accepted it, but soon after, meeting a
poor man in distress, gave him the horse and all its trappings.
Oswin was naturally annoyed, and was not at first appeased
when Aidan asked him if the son of a mare was worth more
in his eyes than a son of God. For a time he refused to speak
to him, but suddenly rose from his seat and throwing himself
at Aidan's feet, said: 'Never again will I pretend to judge of
your gifts.' Aidan was moved to tears, and when the priest
who sat by him asked him in Gaelic why he wept, he answered:
'Never till now saw I a king so humble: it is in my mind that
he will soon be hurried out of this life, for this people does not
deserve to have such a ruler.'

With St. Aidan and St. Oswald, there begins the most glorious century in the history of the English Church: the heathen power of Mercia was overthrown and missions both from north and south spread Christianity over the whole country: by the end of the seventh century, there were 15 or 16 bishoprics established, and in whatever part of England you may live you will probably find that Christianity was brought there by missionaries who risked their lives in doing so. The English Church also sent many missionaries to Europe, of whom the most famous is BONIFACE, the apostle of Germany.

Two episodes in his life are specially worth remembering. In Saxony, in the presence of a large and hostile crowd, he felled to the ground with his own hands 'the sacred and inviolable oak of Thor', long an object of worship: the crowd waited to see Thor take vengeance, but when none came, and Boniface and his monks proceeded to saw it up and build a chapel with the planks, they were very ready to listen to his preaching.

When he was an old man, he decided to make a last effort to convert the Frisians, who had resisted all his efforts. He set out down the Rhine with about 50 followers and they made their way through the villages preaching. One summer's day they pitched their tents by a river, waiting for the coming of some converts for further instruction. Instead, they saw a band of armed pagans, determined to prevent the destruction of idols, and hoping for plunder of gold and silver from the camp. Some of the party wished to resist, but Boniface forbade them and almost all were slain.

So died Boniface, a man of Crediton in Devon, the first of many famous English missionary martyrs, but not before he had firmly founded the Church in Germany by twenty-five years of labour (he died A.D. 754).

But one of the most remarkable things about the young English Church was its service to the cause of learning, which in those days could only come by the efforts of Christians. Canterbury, Malmesbury, and Jarrow soon became famous, and a little later York was so renowned that a great scholar, Alcuin (died A.D. 804), was summoned to the emperor's court when the great Charlemagne wanted his nobles instructed.

The most famous representative of this educational work is the Venerable BEDE, a monk of Jarrow, who has been rightly called the father of English history: he wrote an *Ecclesiastical History of the English People*, which is the source of most of our knowledge of its early years, a book admirably honest, splendidly patriotic, and quite as free from prejudice and superstition as one can expect an eighth-century historian to be. The book ends with the prayer: 'I beseech Thee, merciful Jesus, that to whom Thou hast of Thy goodness given sweetly to drink in the knowledge of Thee, Thou wilt also grant in Thy lovingkindness that he may one day come to Thee, the fountain of all wisdom, and stand for ever before Thy face.'

Bede (A.D. 673–735) was brought at the age of seven to the monastery of Jarrow, one of the monasteries in Durham founded by a learned man who brought there many books from Italy, and there he lived all the rest of his life. All the stories about him are delightful and show him as a most lovable person.

When he was still a child the plague came to Jarrow, and we have a picture of him and his abbot left to sing the service alone: though he was always a great student he was constant in his attendance, and when he was asked how he could spare the time, he answered: 'I know that angels come to the canonical hours (i.e., the seven daily services): would they not say, "Where is Bede? Why comes he not with the brethren?"'

At times he would go to the church and pray alone, and the story is told that one day some of his scholars crept in to watch and heard the voices of angels say: 'Amen, thou very venerable Bede!' at the end of his prayer: this is one of the reasons given for his name.

He says himself, 'I ever found it sweet to learn or to teach or to write', and so he continued to the end. As he lay dying, he was dictating his translation of St. John's Gospel. 'One chapter still remains', said the scribe, 'but it seems troublesome to ask more of thee'. 'Get out thy pen', said Bede, 'and prepare and write quickly'. So the hours went on. At intervals he talked to his scholars, and at intervals dictated. At length the scribe said, 'Beloved master, one sentence only remains to be written.' 'Good', he replied, 'write it'. After a short pause the boy told him it was written. 'Good', said Bede, 'it is finished: thou hast said truly', and in a few moments more he died, whispering with his last breath, 'Glory be to the Father and to the Son and to the Holy Ghost.'

During these years one great question had had to be settled —the relation of the English Church to Rome. The missionaries from Iona, with their Irish traditions, had no desire to be in any way subject to the Roman bishop: they had local customs of their own (as for instance about the date of Easter) and their Church was much more loosely organized: their bishops were not governors or administrators like the bishops in the rest of Europe. And this was true also of the British bishops in Wales: Augustine had tried to get into touch with them, but they had resented his claims to superiority. It was largely a difference between two types of mind, one eager for discipline and unity, and the other more concerned with personal religion and the freedom of a monastery or a diocese to work on its own lines.[1]

A conference was held at Whitby to decide the matter in A.D. 664. The king really settled the matter by a rough jest, saying that as every one agreed that St. Peter had the keys of heaven he would give his vote for Peter and for Rome: some of the Iona bishops resigned, but most accepted the decision.

It was probably the right decision, for churches must be organized and Rome could organize in a way which Iona could not: in those days Rome meant 'civilization' in a way impossible for Iona, but we should never forget that it was Iona which saved Christianity in the north of England, and was largely responsible for that glorious century in the life of our Church. Before we leave Whitby, we should remember that it was there that English poetry began. There was a herdsman attached to the abbey, where Hilda was abbess, by name CAEDMON. He was laughed at by his companions because he could not sing at their 'beer parties', and one evening had gone off to the cattle shed, rather ashamed of himself. As he lay there asleep he heard a voice saying,

[1] One kind of mind produces better statesmen and the other greater saints, and there is need of both in a Church which is to convert the world.

'Caedmon, sing me something'. He thought that he answered, 'I cannot sing: that is why I came away from the party.' 'However', said the Voice, 'you have got to sing to me!' 'What must I sing?' asked Caedmon. 'Sing of the Creation', said the Voice, and so in his sleep the verses came to him, beginning:

> Now should we praise the Guardian of the heaven-realm,
> The Maker's might and His mind-thought.

Next morning he told the bailiff, who took him to the abbess who heard his story, 'in the presence of many learned men': they read him a passage of scripture and bade him turn it into poetry if he could, and 'ruminating over it, like a clean animal, he turned it into most sweet verse'. He became a monk and wrote for the brethren many poems[1] of the Old and New Testament stories and of heaven and hell. He was not only the first English Christian poet, but the father of poetry in England, so that the education which Christianity brought bore its flower in poetry as well as in history and scholarship.

We must find room for a brief mention of two more typical saints of what may be called the Lindisfarne school—St. CEDD, the missionary who converted the East Anglians and became their first bishop in A.D. 654, and his brother St. CHAD, the first bishop of Lichfield (A.D. 669), who has been described as 'one of the truest and purest saints of ancient England'. It is recorded that when he felt himself to be dying he summoned the brethren, saying that 'the lovable guest' who had so lately visited them (for it was a time of plague) had come, and seven days later 'the angels came to summon him to those heavenly rewards which he had ever loved and longed for.'[2] Such men as these, and BENEDICT BISCOP, the travelled scholar and founder of the monasteries of Wearmouth and Jarrow, which he enriched with books and pictures, were worthy disciples of St. Aidan and the glory of Northumbria.

[1] It is possible that some of his lines singing of, 'Jesus, the young Hero, who was God Almighty, who girded himself, and stepped up, full of courage, on the gallows for the sake of man', survive in Runic (Anglo-Saxon) letters on the famous Ruthwell Cross in Dumfriesshire.

[2] Bright, *Early English Church History*, p. 232.

When we try to sum up what Christianity did for the barbarian English we shall see that, though much of the conversion must have been skin deep, it accomplished a very great deal. The original virtues of the English, their manliness, generosity, loyalty, and honesty were not lessened when they learnt other and more characteristically Christian virtues, and their roughness was softened without lessening their strength. Gregory had wisely advised that 'you cannot cut off everything at once from rough natures: for he who would climb to a height must ascend step by step—he cannot jump the whole way', and the sacrifice of cattle and horses, attended by sacred feasting and drinking, passed by degrees into church feasts and 'Whitsun ales'.

The Church had made a united nation, or at least had shown the way to unity: in A.D. 673 there was held a council at Hertford of the whole English Church. This was the first time that any attempt had been made to make laws for England as a whole. Also it was doing its best to educate the nation, and had been the means through which this remote island was united for the second time with the rest of Europe. It had produced more than its fair share of saints and scholars, and when Bede died in 735 it could look back on a glorious century.

In that century too the beginning was made of a system by which in the end the whole country was divided into parishes, so that everyone was (and still is) a 'parishioner' of the English Church, whether he belongs to it or not: the 'parson' is so-called because he is the 'person' who legally represents his parish. This arrangement, which of course took a long time to carry out fully, was another suggestion that England should be regarded as a whole.

But this state of things was too good to last: even before Bede's death decline had begun, and we find him lamenting the good old days when 'the whole anxiety of teachers was not how to serve the world but to serve God', when 'the religious habit (i.e. dress) was held in great respect': 'in those days', he says, 'a man entered a monastery to work and not to rest.'

Before the eighth century was over, the Church and the

country began to suffer from the plundering attacks of the Danes, which went on for nearly a hundred years. They naturally attacked the monasteries first, in hope of the richest plunder: Jarrow and Lindisfarne were sacked in 794, York was taken in 867, Whitby was destroyed, and Northumbria lost its leadership of the country. Farther south, the monasteries of Peterborough, Crowland, and Ely were burnt and the monks massacred: Edmund, king of East Anglia, and his bishop, were murdered in Suffolk; St. Edmundsbury recalls his name.[1]

The man who saved England was the great king, ALFRED, and it is very remarkable that when, in 878, he made a peace dividing the country between himself and the Danes, part of the terms were that the Danish king should be baptized and that there should be one religion throughout the country. We know very little of the way in which this 'conversion' came about, but it does show that by this time the English people were very definitely Christian. The Church, as we have seen, was in a weak state, and had lost many of its strongholds: we can only suppose that the ordinary Christian was able to convince the Danes that his religion helped him to live a better and a happier life, and if that is true it shows the hold which Christianity had gained in England and the effect which it had.

However it came about, the Danes were converted, and within a century there had been three Danish archbishops: we must always remember that, when we talk of the 'conversion' of a whole people, there must be many among them to whom it means very little, but, when all allowance has been made, it was a very remarkable achievement.

Alfred was a great man and a great king: here we are only concerned with his service to the Church. He found both the country and the clergy grossly uneducated as a result of the Danish inroads. In his own words, whereas 'before all was

[1] When Lindisfarne was threatened for the second time (in 875) the monks decided to seek a safer home for the body of St. Cuthbert (a famous bishop of Lindisfarne) and the head of St. Oswald which had been placed in his coffin. After seven years' wandering they settled at Chester-le-Street in County Durham, and remained there for more than a century. In 995, again threatened by Danes, they retreated for a time to Ripon and on their way home were guided 'to finde a resting place for the body of their honoured Saint' at Durham.

ravaged and burnt, the churches throughout all the English kin were filled with treasures and books', at the beginning of his reign 'so clear was the decay that there were very few on this side of Humber who could understand their ritual (i.e. the Church services) in Latin, or translate a letter from Latin into English, and I believe not many beyond Humber. So few there were that I cannot remember a single one south of Thames when I came to the kingship.'

He set himself to learn Latin after he became king; he gathered scholars round him, some from abroad, and with their aid translated many books, including a history of the world, Gregory's *Pastoral Care* (giving his idea of what a true pastor should be), the *Consolation of Philosophy* of Boethius, and much of Bede's history. In days when books in English were very rare indeed, these naturally had a great influence on what educated people thought: he also began the great Anglo-Saxon Chronicle, our most important authority for English history till it closes with the accession of Henry II.

He founded monasteries at Athelney and Winchester, but (so completely had monasticism perished in England) had to import men for Athelney from over sea. By all these activities he saved the Church from falling into utter ignorance and superstition, and we can echo his own words about himself: 'This I can truly say, that so long as I have lived I have striven to live worthily and after my life to be remembered for good works.'

A great change came in the tenth century when Edgar became king and Dunstan archbishop (A.D. 960). At that time there were no monks, strictly speaking, in England: the old monasteries had been destroyed and those which Alfred founded were inhabited by clergy, generally married, who did not live a 'common' life such as Benedict (see p. 24) had ordered. They were called 'secular' clergy, and the word meant that they were not separated from the world as true monks were.

These 'secular' clergy were often neither well educated nor energetic: those who lived in monasteries (the 'minster clergy') lived like rich laymen, and the parish clergy were little better than their own parishioners. We have to remember that our accounts of them come from the monks, who despised them, but there can be no doubt that a reform was badly needed.

DUNSTAN, a man of noble birth, first reformed the abbey of Glastonbury, making his 'family' live together and have meals in common, and made it a school of learning and art. When he became archbishop, he tried to spread the same reform over England, and did a very great deal to raise the moral level of the clergy, to improve their education, to rouse their interest in arts and crafts and to make them once more feel that Christians must be missionaries.

Some of his disciples went much further than he did, and maintained that no secular or married clergy had any right to live in monasteries at all, or to administer the money given to monasteries. They wished to see all monks live by Benedict's rule, or rather by a still stricter form of it (called Cluniac, from an abbot of Cluny who established it in France).

This movement in England started at Abingdon; its abbot became bishop of Winchester, and established the strict rule there as well as at Ely, Peterborough, and other places, saying to the 'secular' clergy: 'Begone, or become monks!' Dunstan did not go nearly so far, and did not expel the married clergy from his own cathedrals (Worcester, London, and Canterbury) though they had originally been founded for monks.

But in one form and another the monastic movement spread very rapidly, and by the Norman Conquest half the monasteries in England were living by the strict Benedictine rule. The north was the great exception, and 'secular' clergy still held such minsters as York, Beverley, Ripon, Hexham, Southwell, and Durham. This made a great change in English religious life, much of it for the good, but there were two dangers in it. The first was that people came to regard the monks as the only really 'religious' people, and the second that as the monasteries became rich they were likely to become quite as 'worldly' as the parish clergy had ever been. Again, it was a great pity that from this time the monks and the parish clergy grew more and more to dislike one another: the monks said the clergy were idle and ignorant: the clergy envied the wealth of the monks and resented their claim to be a superior type of Christian.

We must pass over the brief period when England was ruled by Danish kings, but there is one episode which must be mentioned. When Sweyn of Denmark began his final attack in A.D. 1011 he sacked Canterbury and took Archbishop ALPHEGE captive: he was kept a prisoner at Greenwich for seven months, refusing to be ransomed, which would have meant a burden on the poor, and continued to preach to his captors, not without effect. One day after a feast the drunken Danes dragged him to their assembly, and pelted him to death with the bones and skulls of oxen on which they had been feasting: the final blow with a battleaxe to put an end to his agony was given by one whom he had confirmed the day before. His body was buried at St. Paul's, an appropriate place, as London (like Paris) won its position as a capital by its resistance to the Danes.

We come now to Edward the Confessor, the 'holy but imbecile Edward', as he has been unkindly called, to whom the Church owes nothing except the abbey which he began at Westminster. He had been brought up in Normandy, and was a foreigner in his tastes: the bishops whom he appointed were often foreigners and often quite unfit for their work. He did all that he could to bring England into closer connexion with Rome: this roused national feeling in England. The national party expelled a foreign archbishop of Canterbury, Robert of Jumièges, who was a good builder of cathedrals but a mischievous intriguer, and appointed an Englishman, Stigand. Robert appealed to the pope, who supported him, and this was the real reason why on Edward's death, the pope supported Duke William's claim to the throne, and sent him his blessing, a ring with a relic of St. Peter, and a consecrated banner. This enabled William to claim that his invasion was a 'crusade'; he also persuaded the pope to declare that Harold's election by the Witan (the English parliament) was illegal, which was clearly no business of his: the pope's action was an outrage on the liberties of the country.

With the coming of the Normans the first stage in the history of the Church of England comes to an end. Could it be fairly said that the country was Christian? It had certainly produced great saints and great scholars, and the fact that the English demanded that the Danes should become Christian, and that the Danes agreed, shows that there was something real and valuable in the change. But the clergy cannot have been numerous or learned, and especially in the remoter districts the knowledge of what Christianity meant, either in theory or in practice, must have been very slight. If any one asks that question, it is fair to ask him to explain what he means: Would he, for instance, call England a Christian country to-day? Or for that matter has any country ever really deserved the name? That is not to say that it is impossible for it to happen, but it is worth while to consider both what it would mean and how far we have to go.

NOTE ON SAXON CHURCHES AND SERVICES

We can get some idea of Saxon church architecture from the buildings which survive, though the smaller ones were no doubt built mainly of wood and have perished, and the bigger and more important (as for instance at Ripon and Hexham) have been incorporated in later buildings. The ordinary Saxon church was either apsidal (with a rounded end) in imitation of Rome, or square-ended following the Scottish tradition: the former might have aisles, the latter were narrower and aisleless. Examples of the former can be seen at Brixworth in Northamptonshire or Wing in Buckinghamshire, or Worth in Sussex: of the latter at Jarrow and Escomb in Durham, at Bradford-on-Avon, or Deerhurst in Gloucestershire.

The bigger churches might have a crypt or a tower—usually a central tower: many of them still survive, as for instance Monkwearmouth (Sunderland), or Barton-on-Humber: western towers (as at St. Michael's, Oxford) came rather later.

The greater churches might have altars adorned with gold and silver plates, and chalices (communion cups) adorned with precious stones. After Dunstan's time the arts and crafts were called in to beautify the church. There might be pictures, there would certainly be bells: there might possibly be some glass.

Though the psalms would usually be sung unaccompanied, there might be a lyre to help and organs were not altogether unknown. Aethelwold, the strict abbot of Abingdon, of whom we have heard already (p. 43), made an organ for his church there with his own hands, and two bells which he hung with two others of Dunstan's making. He also made a wheel plated with gold and having little bells hung on it, which he ordered to be pulled round on feast days 'to excite the devotion of the people', perhaps the earliest chiming apparatus on record.[1]

With the beginning of Westminster Abbey in the Norman style a new period of architecture was to begin, and it was not long before the furnishing and the services in all the great churches became far more elaborate than they had been in Saxon times.

V

THE NORMANS AND THEIR PROBLEMS. THE MONKS

So far we have been able to consider the young English Church by itself, for, though its first conversion came from Rome, it developed (thanks to the mission from Iona) a life of its own, and its distance from Italy helped to keep it somewhat apart from the rest of Christendom. It had, as we have seen, its very glorious period, and to have converted the English and the Danes was a great achievement, but the island was too small and its population too scanty for it to be either right or possible for it to maintain its life out of touch with all the learning of Europe.

So the coming of the Normans was a blessing for the Church as well as for the country, but it naturally makes its history more complicated, and England becomes directly involved in all the problems which distracted the Church in the Middle Ages. It is not till the Reformation that the English Church again begins to develop a life of its own.

[1] Hunt, *History of the English Church*, I. 352.

The Middle Ages are extremely difficult for us to understand. They were a time of great ideas about man's duty to God and to his neighbour, which everybody accepted, and if you look only at these ideas, you will think of it as a Golden Age. But on the other hand comparatively few people were ready to carry them out in practice, and it was in many respects a hard and cruel time, especially for the poor man.

Those who only look at the one side have drawn a beautiful picture of Church life in those days, but when we look at the facts we find that this applies only to few places and to particular times. We have always to remember that we know very little of the life of the ordinary layman and that what the histories tell us is mostly concerned with the few who were rich or educated. It was a tremendous task to make the country Christian in any real sense, and we can look at what the Church did without either exaggerating its success or blaming it too harshly for its failures.

As with the Norman Conquest we enter a period of 500 years during which the English Church is very closely connected with the papacy, it is necessary to spend a little time in seeing what the popes of this period were trying to do, how they tried to do it, and why they failed, for all these things touched the life of the ordinary English Christian very closely.

(1) The papacy, since we last saw it under Gregory the Great, had had a very chequered history, but in the eleventh century the same reforming movement which we have seen at work in the monasteries reached Rome, with very great results. The popes embarked on a great campaign for winning the world for God and for establishing the principle that spiritual things were of far more importance than anything else. This meant a claim for much greater authority for the Church, and it was all to the good in so far as the Church maintained a higher standard of morals and of education than the rest of the world.

The great popes saw this, and they did their best to make sure that this standard was raised. They tried to check the buying and selling of sacred offices, such as bishoprics, they declared that the clergy must not be married, so that they should be freed from the temptations of the world: and generally speaking they aimed at making them a pattern of good living, though we may think that they were too much influenced by the idea that the only really 'religious' life is the life of the monastery.

(2) So far, with this exception, no one can fail to admire their object, and so long as their purpose remained simple and sincere they did a great deal for society throughout Europe: it was of very great value to have a power strong enough to keep wicked kings in some sort of order, and an authority which all Europe respected.

But unfortunately they did not limit themselves to these high purposes. Very naturally, but very disastrously, they came to believe that they ought to use worldly weapons to win the world for God, and that it was a good thing for the Church to have worldly or 'temporal' power. So perhaps it was, so long as the power was used for righteousness, but by no means all popes had that zeal for righteousness which had marked the movement at first, and by degrees the papacy became just one other state, with higher claims than the rest, but seeking its own advantage just as much as they did.

In particular, the Church acquired great wealth: it was all very well to say that no monk must hold private property, but the monasteries could, and did, and it is quite as possible for an institution to care too much for money as it is for any of its members. It is a very sad fact that the Church came to be regarded as quite as anxious to get men's money as it was to save their souls.

(3) This is really the explanation of their failure. Some of the popes accomplished great things: some of them took a great part in crusades against the heathen, but more and more they became involved in wars which had no excuse except their own worldly interests. This in the end was their undoing. They came in conflict with France and in 1305 the papacy was removed to Avignon, so that for 70 years the pope was really subject to France, or at least appeared so to English eyes. From this its temporal power never recovered, and it was very difficult for Englishmen to feel respect for the head of a Church which had been so long subject to their enemy across the water. The only chance for the papacy, if it was to reform

Europe, was to remain apart from the quarrels of nations and to keep itself unspotted by the world—and both these things it completely failed to do.

Now let us consider how this new idea of the papacy affected England in the time of William the Conqueror.

The law that clergymen must not marry, and that those who were married must put away their wives, hit the English Church hard, for clerical marriage was common there and had never been questioned. William was quite ready to agree that bishoprics and abbacies must not be bought or sold, but, like other kings, he was indignant when the pope claimed that no layman, even if he were a king, could appoint to any sacred office. The kings felt that the pope was claiming to be their superior, and so in fact he was. His argument was that his power came direct from God while theirs did not, and that he was as much higher than they as sacred things, the things which concern the soul, are higher than the things which concern the body.[1]

With the Norman Conquest England was brought back into closer touch with the rest of Europe and with the 'civilization' which the Church was slowly giving, for in those days the Church was the only home of learning and culture—though William himself was not a 'cultivated' man.

William, as we have seen, had invaded England with the pope's blessing, but this did not mean that he accepted all the pope's claims, and when for instance he claimed to be overlord of England, William answered: 'Fealty I have refused to offer, nor will I, for I neither promised it, nor do I find that my predecessors did it to your predecessors'.[2] The pope did not press the point, and William continued to appoint his own bishops without question.

It is impossible to call William a 'good man'—the cruelty with which he 'harried the north' and the savage forest laws

[1] This was the origin of the famous 'investiture' question which distracted Europe for centuries: how was a bishop to reconcile the allegiance to the king which he certainly owed (especially as he was a large property owner) with allegiance to the pope, which he certainly owed if the pope was head of the Church? It was finally settled by a compromise: the kings agreed that if the bishop did homage they would not claim to bestow the episcopal ring and staff which belonged to his ecclesiastical office.

[2] 'Fealty' is the submission due in feudal times to an 'over-lord'.

which he made were extremely un-Christian: but he did appoint good bishops and in particular, LANFRANC, whom he made archbishop of Canterbury.

The story of how their friendship began is creditable to them both. When William was still duke of Normandy, Lanfranc had denounced his marriage as sinful, and was banished. William met him riding on a lame horse and asked him where he was going. 'Out of Normandy as fast as I can', said Lanfranc, 'and if you will be so good as to give me a better horse I will be even quicker in obeying your command.'

Lanfranc was not a genius or a saint, but he was a learned scholar, a man of high character, and a prudent statesman. Though he was a monk, and sympathized with the reforming party in the Church, he sympathized also with William's independence and thereby offended the great Pope Gregory VII. He helped William to reform the Church, which was mainly done by appointing bishops and abbots who could be trusted to encourage education and discipline. At first these new bishops were invariably Normans, and by 1075 there was only one English bishop remaining, Wulfstan of Worcester. He has high claims to be regarded as a saint, for it was he who succeeded in putting down the slave trade at Bristol, which had long been a scandal, as it was again to become many centuries later. This is an example of the way in which Christian principles were slowly making themselves felt.

If the Norman bishops did not accomplish anything as great as this, they undoubtedly built magnificent cathedrals and abbeys at Canterbury, Winchester, Durham, Ely, Battle, St. Albans, and elsewhere. No doubt Wulfstan, who was himself a builder at Worcester, was right in saying that it was wrong to 'pile up buildings made of stone' and 'neglect those living temples which are the souls of men', but the cathedrals did testify to the greatness of God in whose honour they were built, and there is no doubt that in these days the standard of education and morals among the clergy was considerably raised.

Though William would not accept the supremacy of the pope, he did some of the things which the reformers and Pope Gregory desired: he created separate courts in which the clergy could try moral causes and he forbade clergy to marry, though the parish clergy, if already married, were not compelled to part with their wives.

On the whole we may say that in the days of William and Lanfranc all went well: the pope was prepared not to press his demands: William was honest and Lanfranc was wise. But it is easy to see the troubles which might arise if there should come a pope who was not reasonable, a king who was not honest, and an archbishop who was not wise. The Church in England was soon to suffer from all three.

When William Rufus became king it became clear what harm a dishonest king could do. Bishoprics were sold to the highest bidder, and were kept vacant for a long time while the king seized the revenue, raised the rents, and sometimes sold the lands for his own profit. After Lanfranc's death the see of Canterbury was kept vacant for four years for this purpose, but at last Rufus fell ill, and with the hope of saving his soul, agreed to appoint Anselm.

ANSELM, who was a learned and saintly man, was most unwilling to accept the archbishopric: 'What is the use', he asked, 'of yoking an old and feeble sheep to a wild untameable bull?' But when the 'bull' recovered from his illness and resumed his evil ways, 'the sheep' refused to yield, and finally decided to appeal to the pope. This cannot perhaps be called 'unconstitutional' for there was no settled constitution, but it was certainly a new departure, for the pope had no direct authority in England, but it shows the position which the papacy had achieved, as the champion of justice and morality. Anselm stayed abroad for three years, while Rufus denounced him as a traitor and seized all the possessions of the see of Canterbury. He died in 1100 and Henry I recalled Anselm.

But troubles were not over: Henry, though very ready to help Anselm in carrying out reforms (for Anselm was in full sympathy with all the 'reforming' ideas), insisted that he should do homage to him as king, which might seem to imply that it was he who made the appointment. This, as we have seen, was contrary to 'reforming' views, and while Anselm was at Rome it had been definitely laid down that no layman had this power. The controversy lasted for seven years: there were five embassies to Rome: at last it was settled by a sensible compromise (see p. 49).

We can see that there was right on both sides: it was intolerable that a king like Rufus should have the right of appointing bishops and archbishops: at the same time it would have been intolerable that they, holding large possessions in England, should not promise allegiance to the king, but be the servants only of the pope.

We will pass over for the moment the reign of Stephen and go on to the next great controversy, that between Henry II and BECKET: in this, both sides were to blame. Church courts had for many years tried all clerics or 'clerks'—a term which included any one who served the Church in any capacity, even such people as doorkeepers or singing men. The only penalties which these courts could inflict were penance (which might mean very little), or suspension from office, or possibly excommunication (expulsion from the Church). No doubt the punishments inflicted in the king's courts were very savage, and it was right to wish them altered, but the result was that 'clerks' were often very lightly punished. Henry made the sensible proposal that they should be first accused in a lay court, then handed over to a church court for trial, and, if found guilty and degraded from their office, sent back to the king's court for sentence and punishment.

Becket at first agreed, but changed his mind, and in the end, like Anselm, appealed to Rome: we can see that he had not nearly so good a case. The pope did nothing to help him, and after six years a truce was arranged. Becket came back and proceeded to excommunicate some of those who had opposed him. This so angered Henry that he uttered the famous cry, 'Who will rid me of this turbulent priest?' Whatever he may have meant, four knights took his words literally, hastened to Canterbury and murdered Becket in his own cathedral.

This so shocked the world that Becket's cause was won: Henry had to do penance at Becket's grave[1] and to give up his

---

[1] He knelt before the tomb with shoulders bared and received five strokes with a rod from each of the bishops and abbots present and three from each of the 80 monks of Canterbury. Stephens, *History of the Church of England*, II. 186.

proposals. 'Benefit of clergy', as this privilege was called, lasted for three centuries more, and became more and more scandalous. It was disgraceful that a man should be able to escape proper punishment for his crimes because he had some faint connexion with the Church, and Becket's victory did a great deal of harm to the reputation of the Church as a whole.

But though Henry was beaten on this point, and had to give up his attempt to get more control of church affairs and to prevent appeals to Rome, he did succeed in securing that cases about appointments to livings should be settled in lay courts: if they had been settled in church courts, which allowed an appeal to Rome, these appointments might easily have passed under the control of the pope. As we shall see, the popes did, in fact, secure the patronage of many livings, and introduced many foreigners, who often never came near their parishes. But for Henry, there would have been many more, and the Church of England would have lost its national character. The monasteries depended directly on the pope, and the bishops and abbots were closely bound to him, but the parish parson remained as a rule thoroughly English.

The so-called reign of Stephen was really 20 years of lawlessness and confusion, but in it there was a great development of monasteries: this was natural because, the more impossible it became to live a peaceable life in the world, the greater was the attraction of the peace which a monastery offered. The monks played so large a part in English religious life at this time that we must devote the rest of this chapter to giving some account of them.

Of these new monastic movements the most important was the rise of the CISTERCIAN ORDER which, if not founded, was mainly inspired by an Englishman, Stephen Harding. It is either depressing, or consoling, according to one's temperament, to find that each 'ascetic' movement, aiming at greater strictness of life, yields in turn to worldliness, and has to be revived, probably with greater sternness, in a following generation. The Benedictines had begun to decline, and in 1098 a party of monks who wished to see their rules more strictly kept migrated to Cîteaux. They drew up new and very severe rules for themselves: their garments were to be of the coarsest kind, and the furnishing of their churches as simple as possible: no ornamental sculpture or carving was to be allowed, no triforium,[1] no pinnacles or turrets, and there was only to be one low central tower. In addition they were to place their houses in the most desolate spots which they could find.

The first Cistercian settlement in England was at Waverley in Surrey (1125), but their numbers grew so rapidly that in 20 years or so there were 50, mainly in the north of England as providing wilder and more secluded sites. The most famous of their houses was at Rievaulx, founded under the direction of the great St. Bernard, himself a monk of Cîteaux; it is described as a place of horror and desolation (*horroris et vastae solitudinis*): Fountains was founded soon after by some monks from York, who wished for a stricter life, and both became the parents of many other houses.[2]

They devoted themselves, especially in Yorkshire, to clearing the ground, and became pioneers in estate management, and sheep and cattle farming, doing thereby a great service to the country, but the inevitable result was that they became rich, and involved in the wealth and prosperity which they were so anxious to avoid. It is rather pathetic that the Cistercians should be chiefly remembered in England for the wonderful beauty of the architecture which they developed.

Besides these in the twelfth century there came to England the WHITE CANONS (or Premonstratensians):[3] the CARTHUSIANS, an order so strict that all meat was forbidden, and no talking in the refectory permitted except on Sundays and festivals: and the two great Crusading Orders, the KNIGHTS HOSPITALLER and the KNIGHTS TEMPLAR, the one founded to minister to the need of pilgrims and the other to guard the pilgrim roads. Both had houses in London in the twelfth

---

[1] A triforium is a gallery or arcade over the arches of the nave or choir and below the 'clerestory'.

[2] e.g. Tintern, Beaulieu, Netley, Melrose, Kirkstall, and Furness (transferred to them in 1147).

[3] Another order, the Augustinian (or Black) Canons, also founded by an Englishman, came to England about the same time. They ultimately had even more houses than the Cistercians, most of them small, but including St. Saviour's Southwark, St. Bartholomew's, Smithfield and Christchurch in Hampshire.

century, and the Temple Church preserves its ancient name: the bedesmen of St. Cross at Winchester still wear the silver cross of the Hospitallers.

This short record is enough to show how widespread the influence of the monks must have been in the twelfth century: at that period they were the backbone of the English Church and played a very great part in English life. As great landlords, as employers of labour, as educators, as artists, as relieving officers, or providing lodging for the traveller and care for the sick, they had their share in the whole life of the people.

We may think that they were wrong in believing the monastic life to be the only life that is truly 'religious': we may realize how quickly their good intentions were corrupted by prosperity and power, but we should never forget the great service which they rendered to the country, a service which in those days the Church could have rendered in no other way. We can see the beautiful buildings which they raised, and the beautiful manuscripts which they illuminated to the glory of God, and we should have the charity to remember also the innumerable good acts which have left no memorial, and the innumerable monks who sought and found in the monastery the opportunity to serve both God and their fellow men.

Let us try to realize a little more clearly their way of living, though it must be remembered that, as there were rich monasteries and poor, so there were also good monasteries and bad, so that no one picture can show them all.

Monks normally had their seven services a day, beginning with Prime at 6 a.m. and ending with Lauds at midnight, though the precise arrangements differed in different countries: there were also constant masses, for though the ordinary monk was not a priest there were always enough to serve the altars; as people came to provide for 'masses for the souls of their dead relations', these grew enormously in number,[1] but the ordinary monk was not concerned with them.[2]

[1] In Durham Abbey, for instance, there were at one time some 6,000 such masses said every year. The mass in this sense is a celebration of the Eucharist for a particular and special purpose.

[2] In the following account the details are taken from Durham, a typical great abbey of which full records are available.

The monks might be occupied in any of the works we have just described: on the farm, in the infirmary, at the schools, in the library, or in works of charity. Whatever they did was done by the direction of the prior who, though he was elected by them, had the power of an absolute monarch. There was a prison in which they could be put if they broke rules: a monk who gave a brother a black eye might spend a night there: for more serious offences he might be kept for a year or more in an underground chamber to which food was let down from a hole in the roof.

The sub-prior had charge of the ordinary discipline of the monks: he slept in their dormitory and had to visit each cell nightly to see that all were present, and also to stop them from gossiping: he also presided at their meals in the refectory.

The next great official was the bursar, who had control of all money matters: he collected the rents, saw that the bailiff, or agent, did his duty; and looked into the accounts of the sacrist (who had to provide for the services) and the almoner (who saw to the giving of alms). Each of these had estates of their own to provide for their expenditure, but every one else had to come to the bursar for money that was wanted. Money was kept in a chest with four locks and four different keys, so that it could only be opened when all four possessors of keys were present: this was a good safeguard against fraud.

The wealth of monasteries grew in various ways, besides direct gifts or endowments. Sometimes men would bequeath estates to them (perhaps, though not necessarily, in hopes of saving their souls): sometimes they acquired them by lending money on mortgage, for the monks were the only people besides the Jews who had money to lend and their bursars were shrewd business men. It must be said also that they often secured money left for the parson or the poor of a parish, putting in a 'vicar' (or substitute) to do the rector's work at a small salary, and taking the rest of the endowment for themselves. This is one of the reasons why the parish clergy had little love for the monks.

Then there was a man called the terrerer, in charge of the guest chamber, which was really not unlike a great hotel: it housed rich people on a journey, and poor people also, and the terrerer's duty was not only to see that they were well fed and housed, but that they did not quarrel with one another.

The cellarer had charge of almost everything connected with food and drink, of which more will be said later; a master of the infirmary presided over the hospitals, one inside and one outside the gates; and a master of the common house had charge of the only room in which there was a fire near which the ordinary monks could come. We hear of an annual feast there where 'the banquet was of figs and raisins, ale and cakes, and thereof no superfluity or excess but a scholastical and moderate congratulation among themselves'. Near the guest house was a bowling green where the novices, or apprentice monks, and perhaps the monks themselves, could play.

Next comes the chamberlain, who saw to the clothing of the monks: they were forbidden to use linen, all their garments being made of wool; and finally the keeper of the granary, who stored the hay and corn, and brewed ale in his brewhouse, and looked to all the food which they grew for themselves.

Now let us turn to their food. The monastery estates supplied oxen and sheep, so they had no need to buy meat: their chief need was for a large quantity of fish for fast-days. Cod seems to have been their staple diet, but they also got a large quantity of salted herrings and (if they were lucky) of salmon, which was commoner in English rivers than it is to-day: we hear also of eels, lampreys, tench, pike, and an occasional porpoise.

Some wild fowl might be available, notably geese, and, surprisingly, puffin: if they got partridges or hares, it was probably by gift, and the prior or a neighbouring landlord might sometimes provide them with venison.

We hear of large purchases of spices and fruits, cinnamon, pepper, cloves, saffron, mace, ginger, raisins, dates, prunes, currants, rice, and mustard. But with all these spices, and occasional puffins, their diet must have been monotonous, for salt fish played too large a part, and fish cannot have been as well salted then as it is to-day. They had beer and lemonade: wine only on great occasions, though it flowed freely in the guest house, red, white and claret, coming apparently from Bordeaux, or at any rate from France.

This will give a rough idea of the background of a monk's life, though it is obvious that its details must have varied greatly in different parts of the country. The tone of the monastery depended very greatly on the character of its abbot or prior; if he was a worldly man, things could easily go very wrong: if he was a true Christian, there was no limit to the opportunities of service and worship which he could give to those who really sought them, and in a good monastery even those who had entered it for wrong reasons might easily be won to better things.

VI

RELIGION IN THE MIDDLE AGES.   THE FRIARS

As it was in this period that the foundations of English religion were laid[1] we ought to try to realize what that religion then meant to the ordinary layman.

It is important to remember that the truth of the Christian religion was then unquestioned. Most educated men were ecclesiastics and owed their training to the monasteries, and though no doubt many of the great barons had little real religion, it occurred to no one to dispute the faith, though they might, and did, criticize the actions of some of its representatives.

First of all, then, we may say that the ordinary man could have no doubt of the importance of religion: God was a very great fact, and man had a duty to Him which was the greatest of all duties. That God was great was evident from the magnificence of the churches erected in His honour, and (if he lived near an abbey) by the splendour and dignity of its services: but He was also the Father of mankind for, though the services, in parish church or abbey, were all in Latin, every one knew at least the meaning of *Pater Noster*.

[1] To say this is not to underrate what had been done before the Conquest; but the Norman invasion really made a new nation, and so set a new religious problem.

He knew also that Christ had died on the Cross for man's sake, and though he probably could have given no clear account of the reason for the Crucifixion, he knew that it was a proof of the love of God for man. This great fact was brought before his eyes both by symbols and pictures in the churches, and by the mass which he was bidden to attend. He knew that God forbade certain sins, and that there were certain virtues which every Christian ought to show: the most obvious of these was charity, and, unless he was very unfortunate, he saw this being practised either by his parish priest or by the neighbouring monastery.

He knew how often he failed to do his duty as a Christian and that it was a virtue to be humble about one's failures, and to ask God's pardon, with the certainty of forgiveness if he was truly penitent. Even if this did not appeal to his conscience, there were pictures in many churches of the scene when Christ would come to be his judge, and he was encouraged both to hope for heaven and (perhaps too often) to have a lively fear of hell. How much teaching he received must have depended on circumstances, but he could not have failed to grasp that a good Christian should be just, generous, and honest: that he should live a clean life and not care too much for money: that he should live as in the sight of God, and pray to Him as to a Father in Heaven.

It is of course quite impossible to say how far these duties were actually performed, but the fact that they were universally regarded as duties was of the greatest importance in forming the English character. The English, generally speaking, only became critical of religion when they saw, or thought they saw, that religious people were conspicuously failing to perform them themselves.

But besides these great central beliefs, there was the belief in the pope as in a special sense God's representative, and the claims made for him were so far-reaching that they became, as they have remained, a central point of dispute. It was in the thirteenth century that doubts began to be felt; but we must distinguish between the various claims made for him.

(1) No one at present disputed the claim of the bishop of Rome to be the ruler of the Church; though the English,

partly because they lived in a comparatively distant island, were inclined to resent the interference of Rome in their affairs: it was doubted whether the pope's ministers (or 'legates') had any right to authority in England, but on the whole their influence was used for good ends, such as securing better discipline among the clergy, and this was regarded as a very proper object for the pope to pursue.

(2) It was also claimed that the pope was in a special sense God's representative, and therefore the final authority in all moral questions, and the champion of righteousness and justice. This claim only began to be doubted when facts seemed to disprove it. The pope had supported justice against wicked kings like Rufus: the people generally had been on his side, and had sympathized with Becket rather than with Henry II. But, as we shall see, in the thirteenth century this second belief was rudely shaken, with results which were to show themselves in the Reformation, as the impression gradually spread that the popes cared too little for justice and too much for money, and in particular were not disposed to treat England fairly. Let us look at the facts on which this impression was founded.

John, the worst of kings, quarrelled with Innocent III, one of the greatest of popes: the quarrel began about the appointment of an archbishop, and public opinion was on the pope's side, especially as the man of his choice, Stephen Langton, was an Englishman and well fitted for the post. No one was shocked when John was excommunicated, and even when the whole country was placed under an 'Interdict', it was not felt that the pope had gone too far, though this meant that all churches in England were closed, that the mass was not celebrated, and that the Christian burial of the dead ceased for eight years. John took the opportunity of plundering the Church, which only strengthened the feeling that he was an enemy both to God and man, and when he made complete submission to the pope, promising annual tribute, though it was a blow to national pride, the national conscience was not shocked. But when the barons had been rallied by Stephen Langton to defend English liberties against the king, and had made him seal Magna Charta, it was a great shock to find that the pope cared so little for justice in England that he absolved John from his oath, excommunicated the barons who had signed the Charter, and suspended Langton from his office when he refused to publish his sentence. After this it was hard to maintain that justice was the first consideration at Rome.

A little later, the country had a grievance of a different kind. The popes wanted money for their war with the Emperor Frederick II, and found that England was the easiest source of supply. This was obtained not only by Peter's Pence—a tax of a penny on each hearth, which had been paid for three or four hundred years—but by all sorts of claims, such as 'annates' which meant the first year's income of every bishopric or living, or by special taxes on all church property.[1]

Again, by a system known as 'Provisors' the Pope claimed the direct patronage of English livings, which led to the appointment of foreigners who often never came to England: in 1240, for example, the pope required the bishops of Lincoln and Salisbury to find livings for 300 foreigners.[2] As the weak king Henry III, who was completely under the pope's influence, was also appointing foreigners wherever he could, the doubt naturally grew whether the pope cared any more for the spiritual life of the Church of England than he did for its material prosperity.

Accordingly, when in 1296 Pope Boniface VIII issued a bull forbidding kings to tax the clergy, it was generally felt that he was not defending them against aggression but hoping to keep a profitable source of revenue for himself. Though the archbishop was on his side, the clergy generally were against him. Earlier in the century they had rallied to Simon de Montfort to defend English liberty against the foreigners: it had been a great bishop of Lincoln (Grossetête) who had inspired him: and now they felt Edward I to be a better protector than the pope was likely to be.

[1] For instance, a fifth of all ecclesiastical revenues in 1239: in 1246 a third for three years and again in 1253 and 1257. All clergy who did not pay were excommunicated by the pope in 1258.

[2] Parliament legislated against Provisors in 1351 and 1390. In 1353 it passed the first statute, called Praemunire, aimed at preventing appeals from the king's court being taken to Rome.

The Church was not in the least 'anti-papal', but it was strongly English, and now that there was an English parliament in which it was represented by bishops and abbots it was prepared to support the king. The Church played a great part in the struggle which established the English constitution, and though it was, no doubt, thinking quite as much of its own liberties as those of other people, its prestige and its power were invaluable to the popular side. Its 'convocations' (or general assemblies) had been the model which Edward followed in creating his parliament.[1] With all their faults, the bishops were the only champions whom the common people had against tyrannical barons or an oppressive king, and they did not altogether fail them.

All these events had greatly shaken the credit of the popes: when in 1305 the papacy was removed from Rome to Avignon, its reputation in England sank still lower, especially when England began its Hundred Years' War with France. But worse still was to come. In 1378 and for 50 years after, there were rival popes in Italy and France, and it became extremely difficult to regard any one pope as the representative of God upon earth: it was this last scandal which led Wycliffe in the fourteenth century to an attack on the whole idea of papal power.

But before we consider Wycliffe's revolutionary ideas, we must attempt to describe a thirteenth-century movement which had a great effect on the Church, the coming of the Friars. There were two great Orders, the Franciscans, founded by St. Francis of Assisi, and the Dominicans, founded by St. Dominic, a Spaniard, both of which came into existence during the pope's struggle with John.

FRANCIS, the most lovable of all Christian saints, was deeply impressed by Christ's charge, 'Provide neither gold nor silver nor brass in your purses, neither scrip for your journey, neither two coats, nor yet staves, for the workman is worthy of his meat.' As he said himself, he took the Lady Poverty for his bride. 'The lust of gain' to him was 'the spirit of Cain'.

---

[1] Edward wished to have the clergy represented in the House of Commons, but they preferred to keep their own convocations, which were given in 1283 the sole right of taxing clerical property.

He had spent all his money on rebuilding a ruined church at Assisi, and made up his mind to go out and preach the love and goodness of God. He believed utterly in the infinite power of mere goodness, and sought to win men not by preaching but by showing its beauty in action.

He gathered a few like-minded friends round him, and with the pope's blessing these 12 men set out two and two on their mission.[1] They all gave up all their property, and set out as barefooted beggars carrying nothing for their journey, not even a book. Wherever they came they went to the poor and miserable, to the destitute in the towns who had no one to care for them, and to the hundreds of lepers cast outside the city gates. They were beggars themselves, and lived on charity, but their message was that Christ had sent them to live among beggars, to be their servants and to wash their sores. They called themselves Brothers—Brothers Minor—to remind themselves and others that no one could be less than they. They took literally Christ's words 'He that will be chief among you, let him be your servant.'

They reached England in 1224—nine persons, of whom only one was a priest, though four were clerics, three of them Englishmen, for by that time the movement had developed amazingly.

Outside the city walls at Lynn and York and Bristol; in a filthy swamp at Norwich, through which the drainage of the city sluggishly trickled into the river, never a foot lower than its banks; in a mere barnlike structure, with walls of wood, at Shrewsbury; in the 'Stinking Alley' in London, the Minorites took up their abode, and there they lived on charity, doing for the lowest the most menial offices, speaking to the poorest the words of hope, preaching to learned and simple such sermons—short, homely, fervent, and emotional—as the world had not heard for many a long day. How could such evangelists fail to win their way?[2]

They did not fail: in an incredibly short space of time they

---

[1] *The Little Flowers of St. Francis* gives a charming picture of their attitude to life and to one another.

[2] Jessopp, *The Coming of the Friars*, p. 44. It should be said that some question whether the Friars chose such homes *because* of their disadvantage, but they certainly shared the discomforts of those to whom they ministered.

became familiar figures throughout most of the country. What is more astonishing is that they captured the young university of Oxford, helped by Grossetête, bishop of Lincoln, for in spite of Francis' fear of learning they became a learned body, and produced famous scholars.[1]

In other and more unfortunate ways they fell off from his ideals. They had churches of their own (though always simple and intended mainly for preaching): they took part in politics, and, worst of all, some, as we learn from Chaucer and *Piers Plowman,* actually became lovers of money. But the fact that they inevitably failed to carry out their great ideas perfectly does not prevent us from admiring the greatness of the attempt.

They succeeded in so far as they were true to their founder's spirit and where they succeeded, they breathed new life into religion: by his establishment of a Third Order composed of those who sympathized with his objects but were not prepared to give up all their property, Francis did something to break down the unhappy separation between the 'religious' and the world. He saw the world as all reflecting the goodness of God, all men as brothers, and the beasts and birds as members of God's family—all made for a happiness which they could find if they would simply do His will.

It is impossible in a few pages to do any sort of justice to the charm of St. Francis, but the verses which follow do in a real measure suggest it:

In the greenness of a beechwood on an early-summer day,
    Where the sunshine with the shadow dances,
St. Francis preached to the little singing birds,
    And the little birds sang to St. Francis.

Then up and spoke light-hearted brother Robin:
    'Come out, come out of that pulpit!
You preach because you're earnest, and you want to do us good,
    We sing because we can't help it!'

[1] e.g., Duns Scotus, so abused by his opponents that the word 'dunce' recalls him, and Occam. The great Roger Bacon (who in the thirteenth century predicted 'the flying machine', the steamer, and the motor-car) was a Franciscan, but he was condemned by a General Chapter of his Order in 1278.

St. Francis hadn't finished, but the sermon stopped:
  And says he to Brother Robin of Assisi:
'For men to find light-heartedness is harder than for birds;
  And yet Love can make it easy.'[1]

ST. DOMINIC was a very different man, and the Order which he founded was in many respects different. His purpose was to help religion by fighting heresy, and his friars, dressed in black and white (the Franciscans wore brown), were called *Domini canes*—the hounds of the Lord. They came to England four years before the Franciscans, but we know comparatively little of their work, for they were mainly learned preachers, and learned sermons seldom survive (the most learned man of the Middle Ages, St. Thomas Aquinas, was a Dominican). It should be remembered that preaching was comparatively rare (there was no pulpit in the ordinary parish church); so that sermons, whether simple or learned, were a welcome novelty.

Dominic was a statesman of wisdom and piety: Francis, a saint who was unpractical in the worldly sense, whose life was his sermon. But both did a great work: what that work was is described by a voice which Dante heard in Paradise saying, 'I have raised up my servant Francis to rebuke the avarice of the clergy, to show the uselessness of riches, to set forth for imitation the boundlessness of compassion, and declare the dignity of evangelical poverty. And I have raised up my servant Dominic to be the steward of my word, a wondrous preacher, a subduer of the hard heart of unbelief.'

Some of the heresies against which Dominic fought were certainly very un-Christian, but it cannot be denied that in the Middle Ages any one who tried to use his private judgement was in danger of being denounced as a 'heretic'. A man who 'chooses' (see p. 23, note 1) his own opinion does so at his own risk, and if he rejects the declared opinion of his Church cannot claim to remain a member of it, but many opinions once denounced as heretical have come to be accepted as true. In any case they should be met by argument and not by violence —but this was a truth which the Church did not realize till

[1] J. M. C. Crum.

long after Dominic's day. The most famous 'heretic' of the fourteenth century, was an Englishman, John Wycliffe, whose influence in this country was very great.

WYCLIFFE (1324(?)–84) was a Yorkshireman who was for a short time Master of Balliol College, Oxford, and was called 'the flower of Oxford scholarship' (though he was ignorant of Greek): many of his ideas were to bear fruit in the Reformation. It is not without reason that he has been called 'the morning star of the Reformation'.

(1) He was scandalized (like St. Francis) at the wealth of the Church, which of course meant the wealth of the bishops and monasteries, not of the parish priests. He would have liked all clergy to live on free-will offerings of the people: 'it belongeth not to Christ's vicar nor to priests of Holy Church to have rents here on earth.' This was very unpopular with the monasteries, and with the great 'secular' clergy, some of whom like William of Wykeham, founder of Winchester College and New College, Oxford, were making good use of their revenues; but it was welcomed by great nobles like John of Gaunt, who were beginning to envy the wealth of the Church, much of which they were to secure at the Reformation.

(2) He came to believe that goodness is the only real title-deed or claim to property,[1] and as the papacy was the richest of all institutions, and as the popes were by no means conspicuously 'good', he came into conflict with them. After the Schism (see p. 62) when there were two rival popes, he came openly to speak of it as 'Antichrist'. Though few people as yet were prepared to go as far as this, his teaching clearly helped to lower its credit in England.

(3) He believed the Bible to be the only standard to which Christians could appeal, and denied the value of all rites, ceremonies, and rules (such as the rule that clergy must not marry) which could not be shown to have the authority of the Bible behind them. He wished services to be conducted in the simplest possible way and in the plainest of buildings. It was natural that he should want to see the Bible translated into English, and this, with the help of his follower Purvey, he

[1] His phrase for this is, 'Dominion is founded in grace'.

accomplished, though it may not have been published till after his death.

This was a great event in the history of English religion (and of the English language), and the Bible which Henry VIII was to sanction owed much to Wycliffe: here are a few verses from his translation of the song of Moses (Exodus xv):

Synge we to the Lord, forsothe gloriously he is magnyfied; the hors and the steyer up he threwe down into the see . . . The Lord as a man fighter, Almighti his name; the chare of Pharao and his oost he threwe fer into the see. His chosun princes weren turned vpsedoun in the reed see: the depe watris couerden hem; thei descendiden into the depthe as a stoon.

He was denounced as a heretic,[1] and, sad to say, was bitterly attacked by the friars, who were the soldiers and servants of the pope: it is strange that he was allowed to die in peace at Lutterworth, but in 1428 his body was disinterred and burnt, and the ashes thrown into the river. One of the Augustinian friars describes him as 'the orgon of the devel, the enmy of the Cherch, the confusion of men, the meroure of ypocrisie, the norischer of scisme.'

After his death, his followers, called Lollards, went about preaching all these revolutionary doctrines, for Wycliffe had laid great weight on the duty of preaching. They were forcibly suppressed, some of them being burnt at the stake,[2] but their doctrines were only driven underground to emerge at a later date. There was a prophecy which said that 'their sect shall be in a manner destroyed, notwithstanding at length they shall prevail and have the victory against all their enemies', and this came true.

[1] His heresy concerned the Holy Communion: Wycliffe's doctrine was that of a saint of the Eastern Church, 'we must believe that "this is my body" not enquiring how', and he was not prepared to accept the doctrine of Transubstantiation recently laid down at Rome (1215). (Transubstantiation is a particular explanation, in the philosophical language of the Middle Ages, of the change made in the bread and wine by the consecration.) We shall see that Queen Elizabeth's view was much the same as Wycliffe's.

[2] This punishment had been inflicted before in England, but it now first appeared in the Statute Book (1401) as a law, *De haeretico comburendo*.

We may try to draw a picture of English religious life in the fourteenth century if we remember that such a sketch must be extremely general, and also that it is scandals and offences which are more easily remembered and described than the ordinary life of a decent Christian man. There were no doubt countless people who got from their religion some idea of the true meaning of life, who appreciated its services and accepted its discipline. We are right to judge 'religious' people by a high standard, but we must not think that poets and satirists tell the whole story, any more than novels or newspapers would give you a true picture of the life of the ordinary good Christian to-day.

Broadly speaking it may be said that the popes in this period were more and more discredited, that the monasteries became richer and richer, and that the bishops were more and more inclined to play a part in politics. The laity was beginning to be more critical of clerics, and the pictures of some clerics drawn by the first great English poet, Chaucer (d. 1400), are decidedly unflattering.

But before we look at his portraits we must say a word of the habit of pilgrimage which had become very common: the Crusades were fought to secure the safety of pilgrims to Jerusalem,[1] and English pilgrims made other expeditions abroad, as for instance to the shrine of St. James of Compostella in Spain,[2] or to famous shrines like that of Becket in England, as Chaucer's company was doing. This habit was connected with the worship of relics (bones of saints and so on) which was encouraged as a source of profit by those who possessed them, and thought to win blessing for their visitors.

In Chaucer's *Canterbury Tales* we hear first of a prioress, a charming lady, very well dressed, with a nun as her chaplain and three attendant priests: her manners were excellent and

[1] The Crusades are a subject in themselves: they had a great effect on European religion, but it was only that in which Richard Cœur de Lion took part which directly affected England.

[2] It must have been a laborious journey: a contemporary song says

Men may leve alle gamys
That saylen to seynt Jamys,
For many a man hit gramys (upsets)
    When they begyn to sayle.

her heart so tender that she wept at the sight of a mouse in a trap, but we are a little surprised when she tells so 'religious' a tale as that of the Christian boy martyred by the Jews.

The monk is more interested in hunting than in anything else: he has no desire either to labour with his hands or to pore over a book in the cloister: he is a bald fat man, more concerned with his greyhounds and the fat swans he hopes to eat than with any spiritual matters.

The friar was mainly concerned with hearing confessions: 'he was an easy man to give penance', so that no wonder he was popular: all that was necessary, instead of weeping and prayers, was 'to give silver to the poor friars'. He was well known in every tavern, but had no dealings with lepers, or indeed with any poor people from whom no profit could be hoped.[1]

The pardoner was a hawker of indulgences issued by the pope, the purchaser of which might expect some remission of punishment (in this world or the next).[2] He also carried on a trade in relics, all imaginary ('in a glas he hadde pigges bones'), which he sold to ignorant people, in up-country parishes, getting more money in a day than the parson could earn by two months' work. It is not surprising to hear that, though he sang all the service well, he was at his best when it came to the 'offertorie'.

It must be remembered that Chaucer, who draws all these unflattering portraits, was very far from being an enemy to true religion, as will be seen by any one who reads the beautiful stanzas at the end of *Troilus and Cressida* or the prayer which ends the *Canterbury Tales*. It is shown also by his sympathetic portrait in the *Prologue* of 'the poor parson of a town', who was always ready to visit the farthest in his wide parish, in any weather, and, so far from cursing those who would not pay his tithes, was always ready to give to the needy. He did not desert his flock and run up to London to

---

[1] Langland in *Piers Plowman* gives a similar picture: he speaks of the friars as

Preching the peple for profit of heore wombes (bellies),
Glosing (interpreting) the gospel as hem good liketh.

[2] It appears that it was widely thought that indulgences freed from *guilt*, so that a man could sin with safety.

seek some profitable post, but stayed at home and looked after
them all. His virtues are summed up in four lines:

> This noble ensample to his sheep he yaf,[1]
> That first he wroghte, and afterward he taughte.

and

> But Cristes lore, and his apostles twelve,
> He taughte, and first he folwed it himselve.

We have no means of knowing what proportion of the
parish priests deserved this praise, nor how many of them
survived the Black Death which devastated the country in
1348–9. The clergy seem to have stuck manfully to their posts
and suffered accordingly, the better no doubt more severely
than the worse.[2] Nor can we estimate the influence which
such men had: we can only try to see how it was exercised
and what hindrances it met.

The parson would preach, not perhaps very often (he was
bidden four times a year to instruct the people on all vital
points of belief and practice), and not as racily as the friars: it
must be confessed that the good parson's sermon in the
Canterbury Tales is rather heavy reading. But the people
must have had some religious knowledge to appreciate the
'miracle plays' which were common and depicted all sorts of
scenes from the Old and New Testaments. English drama
had its origin in the Church, and though the performance
might in course of time move to the churchyard or the market
place, it was a useful method of teaching, supplemented by the
pictures with which most churches were adorned.

The parish priest would say mass on Sundays and great
feasts, sometimes daily: he might hold an elementary school,
and he was expected to be both charitable and hospitable.
The parish church was the centre of local life, where all men
met, at least in theory, on an equal footing, and great pride
was taken in its architecture and its furnishing, though it was
sometimes used as a place of business or even as a storehouse.

---

[1] yaf = gave.

[2] In a single year upwards of 800 parishes lost their parsons, 83 of them
twice, and 10 of them three times in a few months: and these figures are not
complete. Jessopp, op. cit., p. 205.

These contrasted facts show how hard it is to form a general picture, but for the good parson it offered great opportunities.

The friars, at first a blessing, soon became a nuisance to the parish priest, and the same might be true of chantry priests.[1] They were at first expected to help in parish work, especially in teaching, but before long they got a bad reputation and on the whole brought discredit on their order.

The neighbouring monastery might be a help and often was, though monks were not as a rule friendly to the parish priests, whom they regarded as inferior in holiness, especially as many of them continued, either openly or secretly, to refuse to obey the law against clerical marriage. As has been said, monasteries often acquired the tithes which should have supported a rector, and put in a 'vicar', or substitute, at a much lower salary: this lowered the parson's position, and left him less money to expend in charity.

It is impossible to deny that the life of the poor in the Middle Ages was deplorable: they were ill-housed and ill-fed: they had few amusements, and, though, partly as a result of the Black Death, and partly through peasants' risings (savagely suppressed), serfdom gradually ceased, the horrors of unemployment began.

The Church showed them all the charity they got, and supplied almost their only interest in life outside the struggle for daily bread, but it is easy for us to see that it should have done much more. The monasteries would never have been abolished with so comparatively little protest if they had been living up to the great intentions with which they were founded: the Church had the position of schoolmistress to the nation (a very honourable one), but its scholars were now beginning to think for themselves, and they found much to criticize.

The Church, as we know, was the guardian of very great principles, such as the doctrine of God's love for man and of the equality of all men in His sight, but, with no doubt many honourable exceptions, it was more intent on preserving its

[1] Chantries were founded in the fourteenth and fifteenth centuries that masses might be sung for the souls of the founder and his family at some altar in the parish church or a side chapel near by.

own privileges than on trying to apply the principles of Christ. 'The love of money', as St. Paul said, 'is a root of all kinds of evil', and all kinds of evil spread through clerical society. Popes were selling rich bishoprics to foreign favourites: bishops were allowing without protest the sale of fraudulent relics: abbots were increasing their wealth at the expense of poor parsons: sin was being forgiven for money payments.

Besides this, clerics were still far more lightly punished than laymen: heretics, like the Lollards, were being repressed by brute force: and the Church showed no desire to reform itself —indeed it hardly could have done so while all the friars and most of the monks were subject not to English bishops but to the pope—and the later Plantagenet kings were in close alliance with him.

The fifteenth century was a period of religious decline: it was not that it produced any great scandals, but it certainly produced no great saints. When religion is not advancing it is going back, and all the tendencies which we have seen were at work. The bishops were becoming a little more worldly, the monasteries a little more idle, the friars less true to their calling; and the chantry priests, the worship of images and the rights of sanctuary more and more of a scandal.

The parish clergy were possibly becoming rather better educated, though no great trouble seems to have been taken before they were ordained: churches were being beautified, and it was beginning to be common, even before the days of printing, for devout people to get hold of manuscript copies of prayers and psalms: and most people were still devout, in theory at any rate.

But if the Church was not getting noticeably worse, the criticism which the Lollards had begun was getting much stronger. The revival of learning, called the Renaissance, had encouraged much questioning of old institutions, and the invention of printing rapidly spread the new ideas. It is plain to us, as we look back, that great changes were inevitably coming. A succession of good and great popes might have been able to direct them, but, though the fifteenth century saw the end of the Schism and the return of the popes to Rome (1420), it also saw the beginning of a series of the worst representatives the papacy has ever had. For more than 60 years, from 1471, there was no pope whose character any Christian could respect.

The higher our idea of what a Christian Church could or should do, the readier we should be to acknowledge its failings: the task which the Church of England had set out to attempt was so great that it may well have been impossible, but in the last centuries before the Reformation it was making little real effort to perform it at all.

In these circumstances it is not surprising that the demand for reform grew, or that, when the Reformation came, in this and in other countries, it was marked by much violence, and sometimes much that was good was swept away as well as much that was bad.

NOTE ON ARCHITECTURE IN THIS PERIOD

The great churches built during these centuries are one of the glories of England: the subject is almost inexhaustible, and here we can only indicate in a few sentences the lines on which English architecture developed. No one who is interested in the subject can fail to find in his own neighbourhood the opportunity of studying it for himself.

The great Norman cathedrals of which we have spoken (p. 50) are all impressive from their noble proportions and the great impression of strength which they give: this style gradually became lighter and allowed of more ornament. Towards the end of the twelfth century the style which we call Early English begins to take its place, with its pointed arches and lancet windows: the tracery of the windows gradually becomes more flowing and less formal, and as time goes on is given the name of Decorated. This style lasted till the middle of the fourteenth century when it in turn was superseded by the Perpendicular style of tracery, the characteristics of which are the long straight mullions of its windows and the greater light which they let into the church.

VII

A DIALOGUE ON RELIGION IN THE MIDDLE AGES

ANOTHER imaginary dialogue may help us to form some opinion of English religious life in the Middle Ages: those who take part in it are Mr. Black, a critical young man, Mr. White, an uncritical young man, and a third, Mr. Grey, who is rather older and perhaps a little wiser, and tries to take a more moderate position.

Black. Well, I'm bound to say it looks as if those old monks weren't any better than they should have been!

Grey [*laughing*]. Very few people are! I shouldn't blame them too much for that.

Black. No, what I mean is they don't seem to have done much good.

White. Oh come! they taught the children and looked after the sick and the poor, didn't they?

Black. I don't believe they did much teaching, except for those who were going to be monks or priests—and, as for the poor, they took a lot of money out of the parishes which ought really to have gone to the poor and kept it for themselves. I don't know about doctoring. I thought that was regarded as no job for the clergy—besides there wasn't any medicine really in those days, was there?

Grey. Not much, and they thought anatomy and surgery rather wicked, but the friars certainly looked after lepers, and there were a lot of leper hospitals founded. I've no doubt the monks did something for the sick when no one else did.

White. Well, look at the abbeys they built: they're pretty splendid now, but they must have been magnificent before Henry VIII destroyed them.

Black. I'm not sure they mayn't look better with grass in their naves and transepts than they ever did before! But I agree they were great builders. All I say is, there wasn't much Christianity in that.

White. I can't see why it was wrong to build great churches in honour of God.

Black. Of course it wasn't wrong: I mean they seem to have forgotten their real job in order to glorify themselves. Anyhow, no one seems to have minded much when they were destroyed.

White. What about the Pilgrimage of Grace? The people in the north of England felt pretty strongly about things.

Black. Yes, I know, and in the west too. But what puzzles me is that if they'd been doing all this good for all these centuries you'd have expected risings all over the country, and you didn't get them.

White. I suppose they were afraid of the king.

Black. But that's just what the monks ought to have been teaching them—to be ready to die for a good cause if they really believed in it.

White. I think you're much too hard on the monks: after all, they'd been good landlords, much better than the average landlord. They did a lot for agriculture, didn't they, Grey?

Black. It would have been a disgrace if they hadn't been better than other people, considering that they claimed to be the only really respectable Christians: I know Grey agrees with me about that!

Grey. Yes, I think I agree with both of you: they *were* better landlords, but not nearly as much better as they ought to have been. That's the trouble all through the Middle Ages —you get people quite honestly professing great ideas and then doing uncommonly little to carry them out—and one doesn't know whether to praise them for their ideas or blame them for their poor performance. That's true of all the Church in the Middle Ages, not only the monks.

White. But surely the country was much more Christian then than it's ever been since? I always wished I'd lived in Merrie England!

Grey. Now there I'm pretty sure you're wrong! England was a very uncomfortable place in those days for any one who wasn't rich, and if it was ever 'merry' (which I very much doubt) it wasn't due to the Church. My real grievance is that they took such a gloomy view of human nature and its prospects: all the best authorities said the vast majority even of Christians were pretty certain to go to hell, and they rubbed that in whenever they got the chance.

Black. Then I'm inclined to say it was the Church which failed, and not only the monks.

Grey. Failed? my dear fellow, of course it failed! But have you ever thought what it was trying to do? It was trying, with very poor machinery, to make ordinary heathen people Christian. It had very little learning: the average priest could barely read the mass in Latin: there was no English Bible to appeal to. How do you expect them to be able to do more than try to make people feel they were responsible to God for the kind of life they led? They did accomplish a certain amount: they protected marriage; they abolished human sacrifice and slavery; they secured a day of rest for people who had to work hard all the week (and a good deal more if you count all the holy days as holidays); they did make it possible for a few people to rise in the world, so that a poor man's son could become an abbot or a bishop. You can't say they did nothing —though, like most of us, they ought to have done a great deal more.

Black. But what about all the scandals? There were plenty of them in the Church!

Grey. Of course there were. There's no machinery for preventing men who call themselves Christians from behaving badly, and we can see that a lot of the genuine Christians made terrible mistakes. But the point is that they did keep the spirit of Christianity alive. We hear all about the scandals, but we never hear about the simple people who did try to live up to Christ's teaching. *Piers Plowman*, who has many hard things to say of all the clerics of his time, says there are three things to aim at in life, 'Do Well, Do Bet[ter], Do Best', and he explains those three duties to be Learn, Teach, and Love. Well, if he learnt that from the Church, he'd learnt something worth knowing.

White. The ordinary chap must have got something out of the miracle plays, didn't he?

Grey. Perhaps—though not as much as you might think, and the Church didn't really like them. No, I think you get a

better idea from some of the religious verses of the time: you
know that little poem which Walford Davies set to music:

> God be in my head,
>   and in my understanding:
> God be in my eyes
>   and in my looking:
> God be in my mouth
>   and in my speaking:
> God be in my heart
>   and in my thinking:
> God be at my end
>   and at my departing.

That's pretty late in the Middle Ages, but there are plenty of
other things like it, though not so good. If any considerable
number of people prayed like that, religion wasn't a failure.

You mustn't ever forget that if the monks and other clergy
seem to you to let the Christian standard down they were the
same people who set that standard up. You condemn them,
quite rightly, for not living up to it: they preached the brotherhood of man, and weren't always brotherly; they preached the
virtues of poverty and purity, and they weren't always by any
means either poor or pure; you can condemn them out of their
own mouths, and plenty of good Christians from *Piers Plowman*
to Sir Thomas More condemned them in their own day; but
they did keep before people's eyes their responsibility for
living as children of God.

Say what you like about their failures: it's perfectly true
(as a learned Roman Catholic said the other day) that the
Middle Ages had developed 'a complicated and decaying
system in which politics, finance, and privileges were blended
with religion'. Reformation had to come, and when it came
it was naturally violent; but you must always remember that
the Church had kept alive the spirit which made Reformation
possible, and that all that was best in the Reformation was a
return to fundamental Christianity.

It doesn't really matter much to you or me whether the
monks and the priests of the Middle Ages were greater failures
than we are, or only much the same: what does matter is that

they kept alive the principles on which we can work to improve our own characters and make an England in which men could be 'merry' because they were trying to do their duty to God and to their neighbours.

VIII

THE REFORMATION

No ONE doubts that the Church in the later Middle Ages was badly in need of reform: even the popes acknowledged this at last, and the Council of Trent (1545-63) did in fact make great reforms—but they came too late to prevent what is called the Reformation, by which about half of Europe renounced the authority of the pope.

This was, and remains, the central point of difference between the Roman Church and the Reformed Churches, and this is not the place to argue the matter. If Christ gave a definite commission to St. Peter, and if the pope inherits that commission, so that he can speak with absolute authority, it follows that all opposition to him is wrong: here it can only be said that the Reformed Churches believe that these claims are based on a wrong interpretation of scripture, that history shows them to be unjustified, and that the pope, though worthy of the greatest respect, has no such right to say what all Christians must believe or do.

Inevitably the struggle was very bitter, and both sides were very greatly to blame, but there is no excuse for continuing the bitterness now. We are concerned with its effects on Christianity in England, and the important fact is that since that day there have been good Christians who have held very different views about the organization of the Church. They differ in the importance which they attach to ancient customs, and they worship in very different ways, but they all agree in the central doctrines of Christianity, unless, of course, belief in the pope is to be regarded as central.

We shall not therefore spend much time over the details of

the struggle but shall try to show how it was possible in those difficult times for good and honest men to take very different views.

Nor need we spend long over the question of Henry's divorce, though that was the spark which kindled the Reformation in England. He certainly wished to divorce Katherine of Aragon in order to marry Anne Boleyn, but still more because he believed that England needed a male heir—and he was quite right in that belief. Good conservatives like Gardiner thought Henry's petition just, and it seems certain that the pope would have granted his request (especially as there was some doubt whether his first marriage had been legal) if he had not been at the moment completely in the power of Katherine's uncle, Charles V. Similar divorces had been given by recent popes for slighter reasons, and the popes of the sixteenth century were very poor representatives of Christian morals.

But first it is necessary to give the briefest possible summary of the actual events concerning religion in the three reigns of Henry VIII, Edward VI, and Mary.

HENRY induced his parliament in the years 1529–36 to deny the authority of the pope, to recognize the king as its 'Supreme Head so far as the law of Christ allows' and to abolish Peter's Pence, Annates, and Appeals to Rome (see p. 61). It also dissolved the smaller monasteries, those with less than twelve inmates.

This latter step might have been justifiable if the money had been properly used, but most of it was given to Henry's friends and supporters, though six new bishoprics were founded—Westminster, Oxford, Chester, Gloucester, Bristol, and Peterborough.

This led to a rising in the north where monasteries were strong, called the Pilgrimage of Grace (1536): it might have been very dangerous if the south and the midlands had supported it, but they did not.

It was brutally suppressed, and all the greater monasteries were suppressed also, their funds being treated in the same scandalous way, and their great buildings largely destroyed.

Henry came to see that an English Bible was necessary for

an English Church: in 1535 Coverdale's Bible (from which come the Psalms in our Prayer Book) was authorized, and next year the Great (or Cranmer's) Bible was ordered to be placed in every parish church. Cranmer also (in 1545) before Henry's death, produced the Litany, practically as we have it now, though it contained on the one hand prayers to the Virgin Mary and on the other a prayer to be delivered from 'the tyranny of the Bishop of Rome and all his detestable enormities'. That the people should be familiar with the bible in English and should use prayers in their own language were great and vital changes.

In belief, the only change was the refusal to believe in the supremacy of the pope: Henry always remained orthodox or conservative on other points, and while he was beheading Sir Thomas More for maintaining the pope's authority he was burning Protestants for refusing to accept the papal doctrine of 'transubstantiation' (see p. 67, note 1).

After Henry's death there were three possibilities: the Church might go still further from Rome and break with tradition altogether, as the Protestants abroad had done: it might return to allegiance to the pope: it might follow a middle course, 'protesting' against what the Church of Rome had added to the faith, but maintaining old traditions and old beliefs. Edward VI tried the first path, Mary the second, and Elizabeth the third.

In Edward's reign the Protestants from abroad got great power, and went much further than the ordinary Englishman wished, especially as he has never liked foreign interference.

Mary, with the help of her husband Philip of Spain, tried to restore Roman Catholicism by force. A large number of English people sympathized with her, but they liked Spain still less than they liked the German and other foreign Protestants, and the large number of martyrs whom she burnt at the stake (including Cranmer, the archbishop, and Bishop Latimer) shocked the English conscience even in a cruel age.

Elizabeth tried, not without success, to establish a Church of England which in doctrine and in practice should be 'national' and yet 'catholic' in the sense of preserving what

was central or 'universal' (the real meaning of the word
'catholic') in the Christian faith. But she naturally failed to
unite either those who wished to go further or those who still
kept their faith in Rome.

It is easy to see how good people could differ quite honestly,
and a few sketches of typical men will help to make it clearer.
REGINALD POLE had always disagreed with his cousin King
Henry, and warned him against his policy. He retired to
Rome where he was made a cardinal, though denounced in
England as a traitor. In Edward's reign he supported an
insurrection in the west in favour of the old religion: in 1549
he was very nearly elected pope, and when Mary came to the
throne in 1553 he was chosen as legate, or ambassador, to
reconcile England with Rome. This was formally done in
1554, and next year the burnings began (there were 75 in
that year).

He must bear his full share of the blame for them. But in
justice we must remember that no one on either side had yet
proposed toleration, and that he did regard heresy as a dangerous and fatal disease. He became archbishop of Canterbury
in 1556, but the new pope just elected was a bitter enemy of
Spain, and even encouraged France to attack Philip and
Mary, so Pole was deprived of his position as ambassador.
He died in 1558 on the same day as the Queen. His career
was perfectly honest, and he was perfectly right to protest
against the scandalous theft of Church property; but his fate
shows how hard it was to be a loyal subject both of the pope
and of the English crown.

STEPHEN GARDINER was another honest conservative,
though he was prepared to yield on points which Pole thought
vital. He tried to induce the pope to grant Henry's divorce,
and though, becoming bishop of Winchester, he did his best
to resist Henry's legislation against Rome, he accepted the
royal supremacy.

In Edward's reign he was imprisoned for refusing further
changes. Though he was prepared to accept the First Prayer
Book (see p. 82) he was deprived of his bishopric and sent to
the Tower. Mary made him Lord Chancellor: he deposed
seven of Edward's bishops, and was responsible for reviving

and executing the laws against heresy, though he did his best to persuade heretics to recant. He died in 1555.

His career shows how difficult it was to find a 'half-way house' when a man once departed from the full belief in the supremacy of the pope, and also that it was hard even for a good conservative to keep that belief in those days.

THOMAS CRANMER became archbishop of Canterbury in 1531 much against his will: he had agreed with Gardiner about the divorce, but also accepted all Henry's laws against the pope, his destruction of the monasteries, and indeed all his acts. For this he can be very justly blamed; he was not a strong man, and those who have never had to serve a king like Henry VIII will find it easy to despise him.

But it should be remembered that he *was* in general agreement with the king's policy: he did greatly prefer the royal supremacy to that of the pope, and he did not believe the monasteries, as they then were, to be worth having for religious reasons. He also entirely agreed that church services should be in English, and did much to encourage this side of Henry's work. He was anxious for reform, but only for the abolition of obvious abuses such as indulgences (see p. 69, note 2) and the superstitious worship of images. This was a clear and honest policy, but in Henry's later years he acquiesced in laws against Protestants which he cannot have approved, and even in the burning of some of their more extreme followers.

In Edward's reign he was able to shape the Church more as he wished, to give it a Prayer Book (1549) ordered to be used by all, and some definite laws, especially as to the Holy Communion: he wished changes to be made, but all things to be done 'decently and in order'. But he came more and more under Protestant influence, especially that of Ridley, bishop of London, and accepted a Second Prayer Book (1552) which went further in the Protestant direction.

Mary could have dealt with him as a traitor, for he had been unwillingly involved in the plot to put Lady Jane Grey on the throne: she preferred to treat him as a heretic: he was tried, convicted, and degraded from the priesthood. Great efforts were made to induce him to recant, and at first they seemed successful, for he acknowledged the pope's supremacy, and seemed ready to go further still. But when brought to the stake he repudiated all he had yielded, and when the fire was kindled put his right hand into it to be burnt first, crying out, 'This hand hath offended'.[1]

His career is that of a weak but conscientious man who was feeling his way to a middle course between the authority of the pope and the anarchy or lawlessness of the Protestants. He believed it possible to defend the English Church not only, as Henry claimed, on grounds of history, but on grounds of scripture and tradition. He saw that the old position of the popes could no longer be defended, and tried to lay down lines which should be both national and catholic. Partly through his martyrdom, and partly through his wonderful gift of writing, he succeeded, and his obvious failings should not blind us to the greatness of the debt which the Church of England owes to him.

HUGH LATIMER, bishop of Worcester, was a straightforward and eloquent reformer: to him image-worship, pilgrimages, and the worship of relics were hateful, as distracting people from the true service of God, and he had no sympathy with popes or monasteries which encouraged such practices. In Henry's last years he was imprisoned as heretical.

At Edward's accession he was released, and preached a famous sermon at Paul's Cross, denouncing 'unpreaching prelates' and declaring the devil to be the most industrious preacher in England: he also attacked corruption and fraud in high places.

Mary put him in the Tower, and after his views had been solemnly condemned he and Ridley were burnt at Oxford in 1555. His last words were famous and prophetic. 'Be of good comfort, Master Ridley, we shall this day light such a candle, by God's grace, in England, as I trust shall never be put out.'

He may be taken as a type of the honest Christian, who, without being a deep thinker, was convinced of the need for a reform in morals and saw no hope of getting it from a Church controlled by the popes. To him, the Church seemed to be far more concerned with external things than with the

---

[1] 'In that magnificent gesture the Church of England revived', Trevelyan, *History of England*, p. 322.

Christian virtues: the practical abuses which he saw made him question the authority which allowed them. He represents the class which was the backbone of the Reformation in England.

JOHN HOOPER, bishop of Gloucester, may be taken as an example of the extreme 'Left Wing' in religion, which was much influenced by Protestants abroad, and was afterwards to develop into Puritanism. He objected to almost all ceremonies as superstitious,[1] and was only with great difficulty persuaded by Cranmer to wear the proper robes when he was consecrated bishop. In Mary's reign he was imprisoned, examined, degraded, and burnt at Gloucester.

He is a type of those Christians who honestly believe that no tradition should be accepted which cannot be traced to the New Testament: this made it very difficult for more moderate Reformers to work with him. Their view (as stated in the preface to the Prayer Book) was that 'the keeping or omitting of a ceremony in itself considered is but a small thing': Hooper could by no means have agreed, and spent much of his energy on protesting about things of small importance.

We may think him tiresome and narrow, as many good people were both in those and later days. But we shall not forget that his honest convictions led him to the stake.

As we have mentioned three martyrs from among the Reformers, let us mention also one from the other side, perhaps the greatest of them all, THOMAS MORE. He was a great scholar, the friend of Erasmus, and Colet (the founder of St. Paul's School), and also of Henry in his early days. He was a scathing critic of the monks and friars and of popular superstitions, but was not prepared to abandon the belief in the supremacy of the pope.

Henry made him Lord Chancellor, and in that office he persecuted the Protestants, though not with the violence of others: perhaps he could not entirely forget that in his famous description of the kingdom of Utopia he had said that there it is 'a fundamental opinion that a man cannot make himself believe anything he pleases, nor do they drive any to dissemble

---

[1] It seemed to him, for example, superstitious for any one to kneel when receiving the Holy Communion.

their thoughts by threatenings'. But England was not to be as wise as Utopia for several centuries.

He was prepared to accept Henry's divorce as a legal fact and to recognize Edward as his heir, but not to deny the supremacy of the pope:[1] he was beheaded as a traitor on Tower Hill in 1535. He was by no means the last of those who found it difficult to reconcile allegiance to the pope with allegiance to the sovereign of England, and when Elizabeth was excommunicated the difficulty became acute.

These half-dozen Englishmen represent the chief types with which Elizabeth had to deal: she could understand them all (except perhaps Hooper) and sympathize with most of them, though her own position was nearest to that of Cranmer. But to unite them all in one English Church and make them work together was a tremendous task, and, as far as the Roman Catholics were concerned, impossible, for they regarded the pope's supremacy as vital, and that she could not accept, nor did the people, as a whole, wish her to do so.

Her three objects were that the English Church should be national, should embrace all honest Christian people, and should avoid persecution (which had proved a failure, though no one as yet was ready for toleration). In her first object she succeeded, but she failed, as we have seen, in the second, and to some extent in the third: for the pope naturally regarded her as a heretic, and when she had been excommunicated by him there could be no doubt that he was inviting, if not encouraging, her subjects to rebel. But if she punished them it was as traitors not as heretics, and that is not persecution in the ordinary sense.

Besides her troubles with the agents of the pope she also had difficulties from the opposite side. Many good and learned men who had been exiled under Mary came back from abroad full of foreign ideas such as those of Hooper, but even more extreme. They objected to surplices and college caps as superstitious vanities and wanted to give churchwardens authority to look after the morals of the congregation, and

---

[1] It is interesting that when Henry wrote the famous book which won him the title of 'Defender of the Faith' More had urged him not to press the pope's claims so strongly.

they held views about doctrine, especially about the Sacraments, which were very different from the old. We should respect them more if they had been fighting for freedom of opinion but they really wished to capture the Church of England (as they had nearly done in Edward's time), and to impose their views on every one else: they made it very difficult to get any uniformity in the Church. What Francis Bacon wrote of them deserves to be remembered: 'Let them take heed that it be not true which one of their adversaries said, *that they have but two small wants, knowledge and love*'.[1]

Elizabeth tried to secure it by demanding that every one should use the same Prayer Book, and though she pleased these critics by taking Edward's Second Book (see p. 82) as the basis, she made changes in it which they did not like but which were welcomed by the more conservative churchmen.[2]

She also demanded that all should accept the Thirty-nine Articles of religion which still appear in the Prayer Book. These were more in the 'Protestant' direction, though they were purposely so drawn as to give as little offence as possible to the other side.[3]

Lastly, she demanded that the king or queen should be accepted as 'Supreme Governor in all causes, spiritual as well as temporal', abandoning the offensive title 'Supreme Head'. She told the Spanish ambassador that all she meant was to make it clear that the pope was not to be allowed to interfere in English affairs, and rob the English people of their money. She did not allow parliament to discuss Church affairs, and herself treated the bishops with more respect than she often showed to others of her ministers.

The bishops whom Mary had appointed refused to accept this (with two exceptions) and were deprived of their sees,

[1] They definitely tried to establish a uniformity of their own, substituting the presbyterian order (as existing in Scotland) for that of bishops; in 1587 a bill to this effect might well have passed if the Queen had not suppressed it. Neale, *Queen Elizabeth*, pp. 309–16.

[2] She altered the words used in the administration of the Holy Communion to those now in use (taking the first part from the First Prayer Book and the second from the Second): and she allowed vestments to be worn, which the 'Protestants' thought superstitious.

[3] Those who study history will see that the authors of the Articles definitely rejected some which would have clearly committed the Church to the 'Protestant' point of view.

but only two hundred of the clergy followed their example, and the Prayer Book soon came into use throughout England. She had accomplished her purpose with really wonderful success, considering the difficulties she had to face, but even so the situation was far from satisfactory.

It was hard to replace so many bishops (especially as nine also had died in the same year as Queen Mary), and the clergy were naturally disorganized after thirty or forty years of upheaval: after a 'progress' through the eastern counties Cecil reported to the queen, 'Here be many slender ministers and much nakedness of religion': and it must have been a very trying time.

In the ordinary parish there would be some who definitely clung to the old faith and the old practices, some of them definitely and honestly disloyal to the queen: those who welcomed the new kind of service would take a little time to get used to it: and there would also be those who complained that reform had not gone nearly far enough, and that, though they had got rid of the pope, many 'popish' ceremonies and practices still remained. To keep the middle path is a very difficult thing when opinions run high and no one is prepared to believe that other people have a right to their opinions.

The influence of Henry VIII on English religion has been much exaggerated: 'reformation' would certainly have come about if he had never lived: it might well have been even more violent, as it was in Scotland. That this was avoided, that Roman Catholicism was not forcibly re-established, and that English religion was allowed to develop on lines which were both Protestant and Catholic, was due to Elizabeth's wisdom, and to her marvellous understanding of her people. The debt which English Christianity owes to her can hardly be exaggerated.

In her first public utterance to her Council she said, 'Considering that I am God's creature, ordained to obey His appointment, I will yield thereto, desiring from the bottom of my heart that I may have assistance of His grace to be the minister of His heavenly will in this office now committed to me,' and her service to religion was by no means the least of those that she rendered to her country.

NOTE ON THE TRANSLATIONS OF THE BIBLE

The translation of the Bible into English and its publication in every parish was one of the great results of the Reformation, and has greatly affected the life of the Church. We have seen how Wycliffe made a great beginning: let us now turn to the man to whom it owes most.

WILLIAM TYNDALE, about 1522, made his famous boast that if God granted him life he would cause 'a boye that dryveth a plough' to know more of the Scriptures than those of his brother clergy who criticized his preaching. He went to London and began his work in the bishop of London's house: some people told him that the English language was too rude to be used for the purpose, but he answered, 'It is not so rude as they are false liars. For the Greek tongue agreeth more with the English than the Latin: a thousand parts better may it be translated into the English than into the Latin'.[1]

But he came to feel that there was 'no rowme in my Lord of London's palace', nor indeed in all England, where the work could be done, so he departed to Cologne, where he got 80 pages printed, one copy of which survives: he was hunted out of Cologne and fled up the Rhine to Worms where he printed 6,000 copies, two of which survive. The bishops in England excommunicated every one who possessed a copy, but they also bought up other copies to be on the safe side, so that Tyndale was a prosperous author. He moved on to one or two other places in Germany, was shipwrecked in Holland, and settled at Antwerp. There he was betrayed by a young Englishman to whom he had showed kindness: was carried out of the 'free city' into the domain of the Emperor Charles V and thrown into prison. We have one letter from him as a prisoner in which, after asking that he might be allowed some warmer clothing, he also begs for a Hebrew Bible and a grammar and a dictionary.

On 6 August 1536, after being condemned as a heretic, he

[1] Compare Wycliffe's remark about French, 'The worthy rewme [realm] of France, notwithstandinge all lettinges, hath translated the Bible out of Latyn into Freynsch, why shoulden not Englische men do so? . . . as lordes of England han the Bible in Freynsch, so it were not agen resoun that they hadden the same sentence in Englische.'

was degraded from the priesthood and strangled and his body burnt. He was not unprepared for such an end, for eight years before he had written, 'There is none other way into the kingdom of life than through persecution and suffering of pain and of very death, after the example of Christ'. His last words at the stake were, 'Lord, open the King of England's eyes!' At the moment there seemed little chance of this prayer being heard, for Henry had issued a proclamation forbidding the translation of the Scriptures. But the year after Tyndale's death he changed his mind, and a Bible, most of which was Tyndale's, was solemnly dedicated to him: two years later still, one was published with a frontispiece by Holbein representing Henry, Cranmer, and Thomas Cromwell all distributing Bibles.

Though we are quite right to admire the great Authorized Version, we should never forget that the 47 people who wrote it under King James kept very closely to Tyndale's version:[1] probably no single man, except Shakespeare, has had so great an effect on the English language.

A great price has been paid for the publication of the English Bible: of the five men who had most to do with it three were burnt, Tyndale, Rogers (a pupil of his), and Cranmer: and one, Cromwell, beheaded. Coverdale, to whom we owe the Psalms in the Prayer Book, alone died in peace.

IX

THE RESULTS OF THE REFORMATION

Now that we have reached the end of the sixteenth century, the century of the Reformation, it is right to try to estimate what Christianity in England had gained and lost. Let us take the losses first.

The first and greatest loss, which hampers us still, is the loss

---

[1] One of the few important exceptions is that they wrote 'charity' for 'love' in the First Epistle to the Corinthians, Chap. xiii, and there the Revised Version has gone back to Tyndale's word.

of the unity of Christendom. 'Our unhappy divisions', as the Prayer Book calls them, make it hard for Christian opinion to make itself felt, and it is only of late years that there has been any real attempt to get Christians again to act together.

Every one agrees that Christians should live at unity, but there are two different ideas as to the kind of unity we should seek. The Roman Catholics believe in what we may call the unity of the 'fold', in which all the sheep are safely kept together, with the pope as their shepherd: 'Reformed' Christians believe in the unity of the 'flock' which, though it may be in different folds, yet owns a common Master. The former idea has great practical advantages: those who do not accept it consider their conception to be truer to the spirit of the Gospel, and think the claims made for the pope to authority over all Christians to have no real foundation. This difference makes it very difficult for Roman Catholics to co-operate with other Christians, for they not only hold strongly to their own view (as of course they have a perfect right to do) but question the right of others to be regarded as Christians in any true sense.

No such difficulty hampers, or should hamper, those who take the second view, for it does not occur to a member of the Reformed Churches, whether Anglican, Presbyterian, Lutheran, Wesleyan, or Baptist, to doubt that any one who sincerely tries to follow Christ has a real right to the Christian name, though he may feel their beliefs to be in some points mistaken, and their practices sometimes either superstitious or irreverent.

From this point of view the loss may yet turn to gain, but by the end of the sixteenth century the idea of toleration had barely appeared, and when Elizabeth died in 1603, Puritans, Anglicans, and Roman Catholics were, as we shall see, bitterly hostile to one another. The old unity had been real, though largely external, and it had gone.

It was a smaller loss that many beautiful buildings had perished, and that good monasteries had been swept away with the bad:[1] and that in the attempt to cut away what was

---

[1] The Church had been robbed of a great deal of its property, which had been given to most undeserving people: but this did not seem a loss to those who thought that its wealth had been a temptation and a danger.

superstitious beautiful customs as well as beautiful buildings and carvings had disappeared. There had been a loss of reverence which it was to take a long time to restore.

Again, the loss of good men was sorely felt: those who felt bound to give up their livings, either from loyalty to the pope or from a feeling that Reformation had not gone far enough, were among the most conscientious of the clergy, and the result inevitably was that many parishes were badly served. Of course there were many noble exceptions. One such was BERNARD GILPIN (died 1583), known as 'the Apostle of the North'. He was a fine scholar, and at first a conservative in religion, but he gradually came to disbelieve in Roman doctrine, and particularly in that of transubstantiation: (his view was that in the Sacrament 'lieth hid a great mystery, rather to be adored than disputed upon'—which is much what Queen Elizabeth thought).

When he became a parish priest at Houghton-le-Spring near Durham, he saw to it that in the 14 villages in his charge 'the pulpits were not covered with dust': he was boundlessly charitable, and founded a school in his large rectory which sent many boys to the university. He conducted missions into parts of Northumberland where 'the word of God was never heard of to be preached' and where vendettas flourished: 'they expect no law, but bang it out bravely, one and his kindred against the other and his'. These were at least suspended during his visits.

In Queen Mary's day he was summoned to London, where he would certainly have been burnt, had he not broken a leg on the journey. He had 'prepared his soul for martyrdome', but before he was able to travel again, Queen Mary was dead.

He made enemies among the clergy by denouncing those who neglected their parishes, and when the bishop showed signs of taking their side against him he boldly preached a sermon in his presence, ending 'I pronounce your Fatherhood to be the author of all these evils'. It is much to the bishop's credit that he was not offended, but promised Gilpin his support as long as he lived.

No doubt there were many parish priests of this kind who helped to make the kind of Church which Elizabeth wished to see: still there was every excuse for good conservatives who contrasted the old days when every one came often to church on Sundays and saints' days with the new state of affairs. And though by the end of Elizabeth's reign new traditions were growing up, this obviously was a matter of time.

On the other side there were very definite gains: to have the services in English and to have the English Bible available for all were inestimable advantages and (though conservatives might hold that the Bible needs to be read with more understanding than most people possess) the way was open for services which all could understand, and in which they could take a more intelligent part.

Again, to most Englishmen it seemed a very definite gain that the pope was declared to have no authority in England. Even those who held that he should have (and indeed still had) authority in spiritual things were uneasy when he claimed to depose a king or queen: and they had also long been uneasy at the constant drain of money from England to Rome, which had now stopped. The best Roman Catholics had for some time felt that the worship of relics, pilgrimages, and indulgences needed reform.[1] As for the ordinary services of the Church, any one who will read the preface to the Prayer Book will sympathize with Cranmer's desire to clear away the countless complications which must have often made them incomprehensible to the ordinary worshipper.

But the greatest gain, though one hardest to define, was the new sense of liberty to think for oneself in religious matters. As has been said, this was still very imperfect, for no one was ready for complete toleration as yet, but there was a change in the atmosphere, and those who did not carry their views to extremes were able more and more to worship God as their conscience bade them. The invention of printing was steadily having its effect in spreading new ideas: some of them were wild, and still more wildly expressed, but it was an inestimable gain that people were slowly beginning to see that Christianity had nothing to fear from the fullest inquiry either into the Bible or into the traditional doctrines of the Church. It was only a beginning: centuries were to pass before this was

[1] Many reforms were in fact carried out by the Council of Trent, 1545–63.

generally accepted, but it was a great thing that men began to feel that Christianity did not rest solely on authority, and that faith was not opposed to reason.

X

A DIALOGUE ON THE ELIZABETHAN SETTLEMENT

WE may make another attempt by a dialogue to show the different points of view which could be held by honest men in Elizabeth's reign, about the year 1569. We have set the scene in Durham where the Dean (Whittingham) was a violent Puritan. Our three speakers are all good Christians. Peterson, a Roman Catholic, Middlemass, a staunch member of the Church of England, and Scott-Calvison, a militant Puritan.

Peterson. So your Dean is back with you again!

Scott-Calvison. He is a godly man, for all that they say he is no priest. Is it not enough that he was ordained at Geneva? There is more true religion in the little finger of Geneva than in all these bishops and archbishops, who have no sufficient warrant in Holy Scripture. The Bible knows nothing save of elders or presbyters.

Middlemass. However that may be (and therein I hold you much in error), the Church of England holdeth by the three-fold ministry of bishops, priests, and deacons, and according to the laws of this realm Dean Whittingham is neither priest nor deacon. But, be that as it may, he hath submitted to the lawful authority of the archbishop, who hath straitly charged him that henceforth he presume not to minister the communion without a surplice.

Peterson. A surplice! what then of the Queen's order that there must be due vestments as of old in a cathedral church?

Scott-Calvison. Nay, those be popish ornaments, and the dean hath well done to cast them aside.

Peterson. But shall Her Highness' order go for nothing?

Say you not that she is supreme head of the Church and that her word is law?

Middlemass. All men know that she liketh not that title overmuch: she took it but that your pope should not interfere with English folk and rob them of their money! Could she but have her way, our English service—save in that one matter of the pope—would not differ overmuch from yours.

Peterson. Why then hath she suffered the altars in our churches to be destroyed? In the church where I served in the old days the stone altar is gone and there is but a table of wood, and they move it where they will for the Holy Sacrament.

Scott-Calvison. To leave the altar of stone was but to foster Romish superstition.

Middlemass. Ah, my friends, these be matters whereon we cannot agree, and I, who honour you both, grieve to see you thus at variance, for I know that at heart you are at one. The one of you resigned his living that he might be loyal to the pope, the other that he might be loyal to the word of God as it is preached in Geneva, and I, who also serve the truth as I see it, would fain be loyal both to Church and Queen. Let there be no hard words between us, and let us not forget that we serve one Lord and Master. For the Sacrament, I hold Her Highness spoke truth when she said

> Christ was the Word and spake it,
> He took the bread and brake it,
> And what His word did make it
> That I believe and take it.

Scott-Calvison. None can quarrel with that, though for my part I hold that we did better to make the Communion a service of remembrance.

Peterson. And I, that in it our Blessed Lord is verily and indeed present. But 'tis true that in the new Prayer Book there is nought to forbid that belief. When the Holy Father called the Queen his 'dearest daughter', he knew that she was not far from the true faith. But those days are over.

Middlemass. But if they be, it is through no act of hers: they tell me that the new pope hath it in mind to excom-

municate her, and bid all that obey him to seek to cast her
from the throne. If that be so, none can serve the pope but
such as will be traitors to the Queen.

Peterson. God forbid that such a trial should come! For
my part, though I may serve the English Church no longer,
I honour the Queen of England, and would fain do so till I
die. I know that she wisheth us no ill: she biddeth us conform
—and that I cannot in honour do—but she leaveth our conscience free.

Middlemass. Her Highness knoweth that conscience cannot
be bound, and for herself she standeth between the old ways
and the new. She would fain have all things done decently
and in order, but she loveth nought that savoureth of superstition.

Scott-Calvison. Would that she were not a foe to preaching!

Middlemass. Nay, that she is not, though she is no lover of
long sermons, but you, my friend, and those who think with
you, seek to exalt preaching over everything; and she liketh
not unlicensed prophesying.

Scott-Calvison. And for that these learned fellows of
Oxford call us 'bruter than any brute beasts'! Must not a
man speak when the spirit bids?

Middlemass. Nay, take not one idle phrase amiss! Were we
to catch at phrases, there be many of your preachers that give
us cause for reproach. What of our own Bishop,[1] who is all
too free with his abuse of them that hold not with him?

Peterson. I honour the Queen, but that blindeth not my
eyes to the sorry state of religion in this realm. Of old the
churches were full at many a time: now men go but on
Sunday: the sacred ornaments are burnt and men mock at
things holy. They talk of communion, yet it is but seldom
offered and still more seldom taken, and Sunday is fast becoming a day of gloom.

Middlemass. Ah, my friend, how easy it is to blame! Your
friends who hold with the mass are not always careful of
sacred things. Here in Durham but ten years past, they tore
in pieces the Bible in the Cathedral and defiled the Holy
Table: and they were men that took the name of crusaders.

---

[1] Pilkington, a violent Reformer.

Assuredly it lieth in no man's mouth to claim that he alone hath the true and catholic religion. Have I not heard you in old days complain of false relics and vain pilgrimages, of priests that cared for nought but money—yes, and even of the pope himself? 'Tis true you spoke rather of his evil advisers than of the 'detestable enormities' such as friend Scott-Calvison layeth to his charge, but the old religion gave but a sorry picture of the faith of Christ.

The Queen seeketh a new order wherein (as is set forth in the Prayer Book) men shall think first of God's honour and glory and of the bringing of the people to a more perfect and godly living. For ceremonies, she thinketh that in themselves they be of little account, yet that a due order and discipline must be kept to God's honour. Hard it is to secure such a discipline when the minds of men are so diverse that our friend Scott-Calvison blameth her for having a crucifix set up in her own chapel, and you, friend Peterson, that she departeth from a piece of the least of the old ceremonies.

She cannot in all things do what she would: she liketh not a married clergy, yet the clergy may keep their wives: she liketh not the metrical psalms men have begun to sing, yet they sing them without hindrance: she liketh not the excesses of those who be so newfangled that they despise what is old.

In all things she seeketh a middle path: of you, friend Scott-Calvison, she asketh only that you will obey the bishop in all things lawful and not seek to overthrow those customs whereby the Church hath been governed since the days of the blessed Apostles: and of you, friend Peterson, that you will not obey the pope in matters that belong to her sovereignty alone.

It is a hard task and a thankless: yet if, as I verily believe, the truth lieth in this middle road, Her Highness doeth well to follow it. Full well she knoweth the nakedness and slenderness of religion in this land: she grieveth that good men of one sort dispute of surplices, rochets, tippets, and caps and say that bishops have no authority from Holy Scripture, and that other good men feel they must hearken to a foreign pope who saith she is no true Queen.

She seeketh not to persecute as do other princes: she asketh but obedience to the laws of England. Let them but be kept, and she will vex no man's conscience. For her part she seeketh truth and peace: she standeth on Holy Scripture and on the creeds of Christendom: she would have all such ceremonies as be ancient and laudable, but she thinketh them of small account so that men seek to serve God truly in their hearts. And for my part I pray God grant the Queen a long life, that the Church which she hath nurtured may both live and grow, for I verily believe that here in England we have in the main put away what was false in ancient beliefs and held fast to that which is true, and I know that Truth is great and shall prevail.

[*Note.* Elizabeth was excommunicated and deposed by Pope Pius V in 1570. 'Ten years later the papal secretary said in answer to an inquiry by English Jesuits that whoever sends her out of the world, with the pious intention of doing God service, not only does not sin but gains merit.' Neale, *Queen Elizabeth*, p. 251.]

XI

FAILURES IN CHARITY IN THE SEVENTEENTH CENTURY

THROUGHOUT the sixteenth century Europe was torn by religious divisions, and it was only the genius and the wisdom of Elizabeth which saved England from those religious wars which distracted France, Germany, and the Netherlands.[1] She had succeeded in establishing a reasonably comprehensive Church but it was still in its infancy and to nurse it required much more wisdom than her successor, James I, could show.

JAMES had been brought up in Scotland where the Presby-

---

[1] It is sometimes said that religious wars are particularly indefensible, and it is true that for Christians to fight one another is a horrible thing. But it should be remembered that many of those who fought in them were at least fighting either for liberty to serve God as they thought right, or to destroy beliefs which they thought dangerous to the soul of man. And this is certainly no less defensible than to fight for mere gain of territory or to support the claims of an ambitious king.

terians were in power and used their power very vigorously:
he did not at all desire that they should gain similar power in
England and thought that bishops would be much easier to
deal with. The result was that when the Puritans in England
made some quite reasonable suggestions he rejected them
harshly and even threatened to 'harry them out of the land'.
This is really the beginning of Nonconformity in England—
based on a refusal to accept the Prayer Book. It should be
added to his credit that he did agree with them that a new
translation of the Bible was needed, and our Authorized
Version of 1611 was the result.

But it will be well briefly to consider the groups into which
religious people fell at the beginning of his reign: each group
had its moderate men and its extremists.

The moderate Roman Catholics only wished to be allowed
to worship in their own way and not to be forced to accept
the services of the Church of England: their difficulty was that
their extreme men, quite logically, wished to restore the full
authority of the pope, and the Gunpowder Plot of 1605 made
it easy to represent all Roman Catholics as disloyal. James
was inclined to be lenient to these Recusants (so-called
because they refused to attend the services laid down by law):
he tried to distinguish between the Roman laity and the priests
who, as being more directly under the pope, must find loyalty
more difficult. But after the Plot parliament became violently
anti-Roman, and any tolerance became difficult.

The moderate Puritans only wished for some reforms in the
Prayer Book (such as the disuse of the sign of the cross at
baptism and of the ring in marriage which they thought
superstitious) and for more provision for preachers (the
removal of 'dumb ministers' as they called them). But their
extremists really wanted to do away with bishops and to have
a presbyterian government under 'elders' who could discipline their congregations, and greatly disliked all set forms of
prayers. James, who had met Presbyterian discipline and
heard long Presbyterian sermons in Scotland, made these
demands an excuse, as we have seen, for rejecting any change.

Those who were loyal to the Church of England only wished
for time to establish their new forms of service, and the

moderate men among them were prepared both to leave Roman Catholics free to worship as they liked and to make some concessions to the Puritans. But when parliament became strongly Puritan, as a result of the reaction against Rome, they were driven to seek the support of the king, and came to form an alliance with him which was disastrous both to the Church and to the monarchy. The less wise among them welcomed the opportunity of trying, with the king's help, to force their views on the nation, and so came into conflict, not only with parliament and the extreme Puritans, but with all those who were beginning to dislike interference by the State with the conscience of Christian people.

Poor James I was very ill-fitted to guide the Church in these difficult days: he was very muddle-headed (as is shown by his marrying one of his daughters to the leader of the extreme Protestants in Germany, while he tried to marry his son to the daughter of the King of Spain, the leader of the Romanists): he loved argument, but only if his own prejudices were regarded as sacred, and his prejudices were very strong.

His action about Sunday observance is very characteristic: he was naturally, and rightly, annoyed by the sabbatarianism of the Puritans, who wished to turn Sunday into a Jewish sabbath and enforce most of the laws laid down for it by Moses.[1] He maintained that 'honest mirth and recreation' were both 'lawful and tolerable', and that healthy exercise was needed by the common people: 'for when shall the common people have leave to exercise if not upon the Sundays and holy days, seeing they must apply their labour and win their living in all working days?' But though he was right in wishing to preserve liberties, he took quite the wrong way of doing so, and tyrannically ordered the clergy to read his *Declarations* from the pulpit on a Sunday. Many refused, and James gave way.[2]

[1] Some of them even maintained that 'unnecessary walking', 'idly sitting' or kissing your wife were offences on a Sunday.

[2] It is sometimes said that the medieval Church encouraged games and dancing on a Sunday: it is true that they came to be tolerated, but this was contrary to the teaching of the authorities of the Church who did not approve of 'vain bodily recreation', called football 'beastlie furie and extreme violence', and classed dancing among the deadly sins.

It is not surprising that under such a king religious divisions became more defined and more bitter. Let us look more closely at the Nonconformity which now came into definite existence.

A Nonconformist is the term used to describe any one who for conscientious reasons will not 'conform' to the order of the Church established by law. These reasons might differ greatly in importance, from a dislike of kneeling at the Holy Communion, or using the sign of the cross at baptism, to a belief that it was wrong that the Church should be governed by bishops, or indeed in some cases to a belief that the worship of men should not be governed at all.

Much English Nonconformity (or Puritanism) was based on the theory that nothing should be ordered which could not be found in the Bible: kneeling, for instance, is not ordered there: bishops are only mentioned casually, without any command that they should continue: many of the commonest ceremonies of the Church cannot claim to have the authority of the Bible behind them. Organs, for example, the Puritans considered wicked and dangerous, though they were able to claim scriptural authority for psalm-singing and for other musical instruments.

This reliance on the Bible was a source both of strength and weakness: of strength, because it gave a definite standard: of weakness, because it ignored all history and tradition, and denied the Church any right to develop traditions of its own. The Church of England was on sound ground when it tried to distinguish between traditions good and bad, ancient and modern, and maintained that the Church had the right to order its own services, though it was wrong to claim the help of the State in enforcing what it wished.

The real strength of the Puritan movement lay in its moral attitude: a poem published in 1622 shows how it was taking new and stronger ground:

> Time was, a Puritan was counted such
> As held some ceremonies were too much
> Retained and urged; and could no bishops grant
> Others to rule, who government did want.

But now, the writer goes on, a Puritan has come to mean a man who is truly religious:

> A Puritan is he, that, twice a day,
> Doth, at the least, to God devoutly pray,
> And twice a Sabbath goes to church to hear,
> To pray, confess his sins, and praise God there
> In open sight of all men: not content
> God knows his heart, except his knee be bent,
> That men, and angels likewise, may discern
> He came to practise there, as well as learn;
> And honour God, with every outward part,
> With knee, hand, tongue, as well as with the heart.

It was characteristic of them to wish for more and better preachers, and characteristic of King James, who hated 'proud Puritans', to ordain that no parish clergyman should preach 'but on some part of the catechism or some text taken out of the Creed, the Ten Commandments, or the Lord's Prayer', and that only bishops and deans were to preach on deep points of theology.

What was more important was that at this very time the Court was corrupt and drunken, so that the Puritan movement became more and more critical of the king, at the very time when the Church was coming more and more to rely on him to defend its rights against parliament. Religion and politics were becoming dangerously mixed.

The strength of Puritanism lay in the fact that the Puritans seemed to care more for morality than the official Church did. Baxter's father was called 'Puritan, Precisian, and Hypocrite' for reading scripture, having family prayers, and reproving drunkards and swearers, and 'talking sometimes a few words of Scripture and the life to come': Sir Thomas Hutchinson was branded with the name Puritan—'the reproach of the world, though the glory of good men'—because he favoured humble preachers of goodness—'oppressed saints and honest people'. Though naturally some such preachers were hypocrites, and adopted 'a whining fashion of speaking' (so that one of them was admonished by a godly gentlewoman 'to live like a good man, but to speak like a man'), they were allowed to become in the public view the champions of morality, and it was to take the Church two centuries to recover the ground it then lost.

The weakness of Puritanism came from its close association with Calvinism, for Calvin taught a form of predestination which seemed to most Englishmen to deny the freedom of man's will, if not the justice of God,[1] and also a form of presbyterian government which, though it appealed to the Scots, was never at all popular in England. Later on in the century the Puritans were to show themselves quite as ready as the Church to rely on the support of the State, with results equally disastrous to their cause. The Puritans were, if anything, even more intolerant than any one else: it was under Abbot, a Puritan archbishop, that the last heretics were burnt in 1612, and under the Commonwealth there was far less liberty than under Laud. The chief lesson of the seventeenth century religion was that for a religious body to ally itself with a political party is fatal to its life. But the lesson was only slowly learnt.

By the time Charles I came to the throne religious differences had become more acute, and though Charles was a much better man than his father he was not much wiser than he. It is true that the Court ceased to be scandalous, but on the other hand his wife was a Roman Catholic, and, as she was allowed her own priest, it was easy, though quite untrue, to suggest that he was himself disloyal to the English Church. In fact he was devotedly attached to it, and lost much of his popularity by allowing, or encouraging, Laud (archbishop of Canterbury from 1633) to enforce its regulations. Their object (as stated in the Declaration printed in the Prayer Book before the Articles of Religion) was a noble one, 'to maintain the Church, in the Unity of true Religion; and in the Bond of Peace, and not to suffer unnecessary Disputations, Altercations, or Questions to be raised, which may nourish Faction both in the Church and Commonwealth', but their methods were very unfortunate, and by the severe use of the law

---

[1] In Laud's words 'It makes God, the God of all mercies, to be the most fierce and unreasonable tyrant in the world'. The word 'predestination' means that everything is foreordained by God, and this clearly may be taken in a sense which leaves no room at all for freewill.

encouraged the 'curious and unhappy differences' which they hoped to remove. They offended lazy clergymen as well as the Puritans whom they tried to harry into conformity with ceremonies which they thought superstitious (see pp. 84 and 100). It was by the attempt to impose a Prayer Book, known as 'Laud's Liturgy'[1], on Scotland where Calvinism was strong, that they first provoked armed rebellion.

But if Charles was unwise and intolerant, parliament was at least equally intolerant and equally unwise.[2] They passed in 1643 a bill abolishing bishops, and accepted the Solemn League and Covenant with the Scots, agreeing to reform the Church 'according to the Word of God and the example of the best reformed churches'.[3] The use of the Prayer Book was forbidden and many Episcopalian clergy turned out: Charles could probably have saved his life if he had agreed to accept this situation: that is the justification for calling him 'Charles the Martyr'. Worse was to follow: from 1653 to 1660 liberty of religion (allowed to all believers in the Trinity and the Scriptures) was denied to Papists and Episcopalians: all the latter were removed from their livings and in many cases suffered great hardship: there was much wanton destruction in the churches, especially of carved woodwork and glass:[4] observance of Christmas Day was forbidden, and a congregation which met secretly to celebrate it was imprisoned. The Roman Catholics suffered even more, and the last man executed in England for holding that faith died in 1654. Though Cromwell was personally tolerant he had no

[1] It should be observed that this was not the English Prayer Book but one drawn up by two Scottish bishops, and that it gave offence largely because it prescribed set forms of prayer.

[2] In 1629 the House of Commons had passed a resolution aimed at establishing Calvinism, denouncing any one who opposed it as 'a capital enemy to this kingdom and commonwealth'.

[3] The Scots would have liked them to establish Presbyterianism in England, but parliament did not wish to surrender its power and the 'Independents' (who were represented by Cromwell) were inclined to hold that no congregation ought to have authority over any other. Presbyterianism was established in a half-hearted way, but only took firm hold in London and some parts of Lancashire.

[4] The Puritans habitually destroyed crucifixes and even crosses: any representation of cherubs and angels was an abomination to them, though they were more tolerant of devils in glass, wood, or stone.

official mercy for Anglicans, Roman Catholics, Quakers, or Unitarians.

It is not surprising, though it is very regrettable, that at the Restoration in 1660 there should have been violent retaliation. Charles II had promised that 'no man shall be disquieted or called in question for differences of opinion in matters of religion which do not disturb the peace of the kingdom', but parliament would not let him keep his word, and after the breakdown of an attempt, at the Savoy Conference in 1661, to see whether Puritans and Presbyterians could be induced to accept the Prayer Book, it proceeded to avenge the sufferings of the Church. Two thousand Puritan clergy were expelled without compensation, and a series of discreditable acts was passed preventing attendance at non-Anglican services, forbidding expelled ministers to come within five miles of a town or of their old parishes,[1] and ordering all members of corporations to receive the Sacrament according to the rites of the Church of England.

This legislation, and other similar legislation against Roman Catholics which followed later, was the work of parliament, not of the king or the bishops, though they did nothing to prevent it: the best that can be said is that it was not consistently carried out, but this does not excuse its wholly unchristian character.

Later attempts at toleration by Charles and James II were rightly suspect as being designed to help the restoration of Roman Catholicism. When James II in 1687 issued a Declaration of Indulgence giving freedom of worship to all, wise Nonconformists, like Baxter, refused to trust him or welcome it, and when next year he ordered it to be read in the churches, the famous Seven Bishops refused: only few clergy read it and the Bishops when tried were triumphantly acquitted. The result was the invitation to William and Mary and the flight of James.

With the new reign we see the slow beginnings of toleration, but as we look back on the century as a whole we see a most

---

[1] Baxter loved to point out that at the very time when this act was being passed the Nonconformists were diligently ministering in London during its sufferings from the Plague and the Fire (1665–6).

depressing picture of the lack of Christian charity, and of the
misuse of power by men many of whom were, in their different
ways, sincere followers of Christ.

XII

SEVENTEENTH-CENTURY RELIGION AT ITS BEST

LET us turn from this gloomy record to see how in this
century the Christian life was lived by men of various types,
and to notice their real unity of spirit.

LANCELOT ANDREWES (1555–1626) successively bishop of
Chichester, Ely, and Winchester, shows the Church of
England at its best. He maintained that it was a truly Catholic
Church, preserving all the beliefs which had been held
'always, everywhere, by all Christians', whereas the characteristically Roman doctrines dated only from the Middle Ages.
He showed that the 'royal supremacy' did not set up the king
as a pope (as the Roman Catholics maintained), but only gave
him ecclesiastical supremacy, while supremacy in spiritual
things, such as matters of faith and worship, reverted to the
bishops and archbishops. But he was the one man with whom
all Roman Catholics could argue without loss of temper, and
when he failed to convince 'recusants' he did his best to secure
better treatment for them. Similarly, he was always courteous
in his dealings with the Puritans, and he did a great deal to
keep religious controversies from becoming vulgar and
abusive.

He had strong feelings about the need for reverence in
worship, and in his private chapel restored various ceremonies to ensure it, but he made no attempt to force his views
upon others, and the result was that his influence was great in
promoting a higher standard in such matters. So great was
the respect for him that neither his ritual nor his character

was ever attacked, and he is the best personal link between the old and the new order of religion in England.[1]

He left behind him a little book of Private Prayer, and a few sentences from it will help to show his character:

> Thou who willest us to make return to our benefactors, remember, Lord, for good all from whom I have received good: keep them alive that they may be blessed upon earth, and deliver them not into the will of their enemies. Thou who wouldest that our righteousness exceed the righteousness of sinners, grant me, Lord, to love those who love me; my own friend, and my father's friend, and my friend's children never to forsake. Thou who wouldest that we overcome evil with good, and pray for those who persecute us, have pity on mine enemies, Lord, as on myself; and lead them together with me to thy heavenly kingdom.

If WILLIAM LAUD (1573–1645), who was Andrewes' pupil' had had his master's character, the whole history of the Church of England might have been different. It is a real tragedy, for his aims were very great and the causes of his failure comparatively small.

'He had at heart the ideal of a united England with a Church at once Catholic, Scriptural, Apostolic, free from superstition, yet reverently retaining all that was primitive; a resting place for all men of enlightenment; a model of piety and devotion to a distracted world.'[2] As he said himself on the scaffold, 'This poor Church of England hath been a shelter to other neighbouring Churches when storms have driven upon them.' So far was he from being by nature intolerant that he said, 'I will never take it upon me to express that opinion (the denial of the foundation only excepted) which may shut any Christian, even the meanest, out of heaven.'

He believed that, if the services of the Church, according to the Prayer Book, were fully and fairly performed, they would of themselves attract and convince, for men would soon

---

[1] A story told of him and Neile, bishop of Durham, shows his gentle humour. The king asked them both if he could not take his subjects' money without 'this formality of parliament'. Neile enthusiastically agreed, and James turned to Andrewes: 'I think, sir', he replied, 'that it is lawful for you to take my brother Neile's money, since he offers it.'

[2] Creighton, *Historical Lectures*, p. 176.

understand and love them. The reason why people 'think meanly of the Church of England' was that 'the external worship of God was so lost, and the churches themselves suffered to lie in such a base and slovenly fashion in most places of the kingdom.'

So he set himself to teach by the eye, and to restore throughout the country the decency of worship which men like Andrewes valued, and so far he must command our sympathy. When he became bishop of London, St. Paul's had long been used like an alley on 'Change: we read of fighting cocks in some parish churches: of others where the congregation lounged on the altars, and of a dog which carried off the bread prepared for Sacrament. It was by no means a mere love of ritual which made him desire to see the holy table removed to the east end of the church and fenced with a decent rail.

But his methods were all wrong: he had no tact and little knowledge of human nature: 'he did court persons too little,' as Clarendon says, 'and did not consider enough what men said or were like to say of him.' He thought that the way to prove a thing was reasonable was to enforce it, and he issued orders like a colonel or a schoolmaster instead of trying to win sympathy.

Again, he identified Church and State, and himself held office as a State official. The Court of High Commission set itself to reform morality and did not hesitate to punish 'persons of honour and great quality': it also dealt with blasphemy and sacrilege, but its methods (like those of other law courts of the time) were unfair, and the blame fell on the Church and on Laud, 'the little meddling hocus-pocus'.

So it came about that, much though he did to restore reverence and decency of worship, as well as to improve public morals, he was bitterly hated, by the Puritans for one reason, by the slacker clergy for another, and by the average Englishman for yet a third. He was over-hasty and over-punctilious, and never succeeded in kindling enthusiasm in others; and he was severe in punishing libellous attacks on himself.

But such faults as these do nothing to justify his brutal murder by parliament in 1645, perhaps the greatest crime in its history. As he said on the scaffold, 'I am not only the first

Archbishop, but the first man, that hath ever died by an ordinance in Parliament.' In that same speech he protested his complete loyalty to the Church of England:

In that profession I have lived, and in that I come now to die. . . . What clamours and slanders I have endured for labouring to keep a uniformity in the external service of God, all men know and I have abundantly felt. I forgive all the world, all and every of those bitter enemies which have persecuted me: and humbly desire to be forgiven of God first, and then of every man whether I have offended him or not, if he do but conceive that I have . . . The Lord receive my soul, and bless this kingdom with peace and plenty, and with brotherly love and charity, that there may not be this effusion of Christian blood amongst them, for Jesus Christ His sake, if it be Thy will.

GEORGE HERBERT (1593–1632) in his short ministry showed what a parish priest trained on Laud's principles could do. When he 'changed his sword and silk clothes into a canonical coat' and became rector of Bemerton, he repaired the church and set down in a little book called *The Country Parson* his ideas of the way in which his duties should be discharged. He was to be 'holy, just, prudent, temperate, bold, grave in all his wayes', careful to avoid luxury, and 'very strict in keeping his word', for country people 'will not believe him in the pulpit, whom they cannot trust in his Conversation.' He will use 'all possible reverence' in his public prayers, and will exact the same of his people, 'by no means enduring either talking, or sleeping, or gazing, or leaning or halfe-kneeling': nor will he tolerate lax behaviour on the part of gentry or nobility 'who sometimes make it a piece of state not to come at the beginning of service with their poor neighbours.' 'The pulpit is his joy and throne'—a sentiment which the Puritans would have endorsed—'he exceeds not an hour in preaching', which most Puritans would have thought insufficient. He makes his house 'a copy and modell for his Parish': 'his fare is plain, and common, but wholesome': he is careful to observe abstinence on a Friday. He is a man of courtesy and charity.

As for his church, he takes care 'that all things there be decent, and befitting his Name by which it is called . . .

desiring to keep the middle way between superstition, and slovenlinesse': at great festivals his church is 'strawed, and stuck with boughs, and perfumed with incense.' 'He useth, and preferreth, the ordinary Church-Catechism, partly for obedience to Authority, partly for uniformity sake, that the same common truths may be every where professed'. He celebrates the Communion, 'if not duly once a month, yet at least five or six times in the year', taking all possible pains that those who come are well prepared. He 'desires to be all to his Parish, and not onely a Pastour, but a Lawyer also, and a Phisician': he is regular in visiting the sick, and if he ever has to rebuke or punish, esteems the delinquent not 'for an enemy, but as a brother still'.

Herbert wrote many admirable religious poems and hymns, the most famous of which begins

> Teach me, my God and King,
>   In all things thee to see,
>   And what I do in any thing,
> To do it as for thee.

Izaak Walton's delightful life of him ends with these words:

Thus he liv'd, and thus he dy'd like a saint, unspotted of the World, full of Alms-deeds, full of Humility, and all the examples of a vertuous life . . . I have but this to say more of him: That if Andrew Melvin dyed before him, then George Herbert dyed without an enemy. I wish (if God shall be so pleased) that I may be so happy as to dye like him.

NICHOLAS FERRAR (1591–1637) and his family—mother, son, and daughter—lived at Little Gidding, in what their enemies called 'a Protestant nunnery', a life of simple Christian piety which is very attractive. They fasted, they prayed, they cared for the poor: they restored churches: they translated books: they practised the art of bookbinding. Twice daily they attended common prayer in church: twice daily they prayed together at home: all day and all night one of them was engaged in some private holy exercise.[1]

In their parlour hung a notice, 'He that will demonstrate

---

[1] 'They kept sentinel at all hours and seasons to expect the second coming of the Lord Jesus.'

that which is more perfect and seek to make us better, is welcome as an angel of God. He, that, by cheerful participating and approbation of that which is good, confirms us in the same, is welcome as a Christian friend.'

The bishop approved them: King Charles visited them three times: but the parliamentary soldiers sacked church and house in 1646 and the little community came to an end.

SIR THOMAS BROWNE (1605–82), the learned author of *Religio Medici*, was a loyal member of the English Church, and puts its principles simply. He is sorry, he says, that the pope can allow him no better name than heretic, but has no desire to retaliate in the same way:

I condemn not all things in the Council of Trent, nor approve all things in the Synod of Dort.[1] . . . Where the Scripture is silent, the Church is my text: where there is a joynt silence of both, I borrow not the rules of my religion from Rome or Geneva, but the dictates of my own reason . . . All who suffer in the name of religion are not martyrs, and many canonized on earth will never be saints in heaven: that wise heathen Socrates may in the eyes of God be a better martyr than they.

His faith was based on two books, that of God and that of Nature. Each night he repeated his 'colloquy with God', for 'sleep is so like death I dare not trust it without my Prayers': the colloquy begins

> The night is come, like to the day,
> Depart not, Thou, great God, away.

This is the Dormative I take to bedward: I need no other laudanum than this to make me sleep: after which I close my eyes in serenity, content to take my leave of the Sun, and sleep unto the Resurrection.

JEREMY TAYLOR (1613–67), bishop of Down, was said by his successor to have had 'the good humour of a gentleman, the eloquence of an orator, the fancy of a poet, the acuteness of a schoolman, the profoundness of a philosopher, the wisdom of a chancellor, the sagacity of a prophet, the reason of an angel and the piety of a saint'.

His *Holy Living and Dying*, which maintained the principal place in the study of almost every elegant and high divine and

[1] The Synod of Dort was an extremely Protestant gathering.

'stood on the advanced shelves on glass cupboards of the
lady's closets', goes far to justify this praise. A few quotations
will show that a bishop trained in the school of Laud was by
no means concerned only with outward things, but rather (in
a phrase which he perhaps coined) with 'the practice of the
presence of God'.

We are of the same household with God. He is with us in our
natural actions to preserve us: in our recreations to restrain us: and
if we walk with God in all His ways as He walks with us in all ours,
we shall find perpetual reasons to enable us to keep that rule of
God 'Rejoice in the Lord always, and again I say, rejoice'.

Fear no man's person in the doing of your duty wisely, and
according to the laws, remembering always that a servant of God
can be no more hurt by all the powers of wickedness than by the
noise of a fly's wing, or the chirping of a sparrow.

Let men not be hasty in calling every disliked opinion by the
name of heresy: and when they have resolved that they will call it
so, let them use the erring person like a brother, not beat him like
a dog, nor convince him with a gibbet.

God, who in mercy and wisdom governs the world, would never
have suffered so many sadnesses . . . but that He intends they
should be the seminary of comfort, the nursery of virtue, the exercise
of wisdom, the trial of patience, the gate of glory.

If our actions be designed well, they are likely to end well: for
in the service of God a golden head shall never have feet of clay.

The life of RICHARD BAXTER (1615–91), 'the Saint of
Puritanism', shows how narrow was the gap between the
good Anglican priest and the good Puritan pastor. As a boy
he suffered from the poor character of the clergy who had to
teach him: 'I was in my childhood first bred up under the
School and Church teaching of eight several men of whom
only two preached once a month and the rest were but readers
of the Liturgie and most of very scandalous lives.' But,
having from his youth been anxious to 'communicate his
apprehension of the Matters of another World to such
ignorant, presumptuous, careless sinners as the World abound-
eth with', he was ordained by the bishop of Worcester.

He had no doubts as to the general merits of Episcopacy,
and, with regard to the special points against which Puritans

protested, he thought kneeling 'lawful', he 'more doubted of' the use of the surplice, made no scruple of the ring in marriage, but resolved never to use the cross in baptism: the Prayer Book seemed to him to have nothing in it which should make the use of it 'unlawful to them that have not liberty to do better'.[1] This in the main was the position which he held to the end. He thought that the bitterness of Puritan attacks on the bishops was 'as contrary to Christian charity on one side as Persecution on the other', and tried to restrain it.

After some time at Dudley and Bridgnorth, he was chosen in 1641 as 'Lecturer' at Kidderminster, where the vicar and his curates were men of poor character: 'Lecturers', who stood for the moral aspect of worship as distinct from the ceremonial, were a characteristically Puritan creation which Laud had attempted to suppress. So began a ministry which (with a five-year interval, during most of which Baxter served as a chaplain with the parliamentary army) lasted till 1660 and had astonishing results.

In 1647, when he returned from the war, he became vicar of Kidderminster, though it was characteristic of him that he allowed the old vicar to keep his house and some of his salary, and even to use the (illegal) book of Common Prayer for those who wished it.

Here is a brief summary of his ministry taken from his own account.

After the war I preached but once on the Lord's Day, and once every Thursday. Every Thursday evening my neighbours met at my house and proposed what doubts any of them had about the sermon . . . once a week some of the younger sort spent three hours praying together: every Saturday night they met at some of their houses to repeat the sermon of the last Lord's Day and to pray and prepare themselves for the following day. . . . Two days every week my assistant and myself took fourteen families between us for private catechising. I spent about an hour with a family. Besides all this I was forced for five or six years by the people's necessity to practise physick. . . . Every first Wednesday of the month was our monthly meeting for parish discipline, and every first Thursday was

[1] At the time of the Savoy Conference he said he was 'not of their mind who charged the Common Prayer with false Doctrine, or Idolatry, or false Worship'. Its defects in his view were disorder and defectiveness.

the Ministers' meeting for discipline and disputation. . . . Blessed be the God of mercies that gave me after wars and sickness fourteen years liberty in such sweet employment.

The effect of his labours was marked. 'When I came thither first there was about one Family in a Street that worshipped God and called on His name, and when I came away there were some Streets where there was not past one Family in the side of a Street that did not so . . . the zeal and knowledge of this poor People provoked many in other parts of the Land.' His influence over the 600 Church members who accepted his government was very great, but there were 1,400 who did not: his difficulty was that he was trying to combine the 'parochial' idea, which assumes that the parson is responsible for all his parish, with the idea that the minister is only concerned with the 'elect' or the 'saved', a much less exacting task.

Throughout his life his object was work for a united Church: his favourite motto was that of Athanasius: 'in necessary things, unity; in doubtful things, liberty; in all things, charity'[1]. He formed the Worcestershire Association on the basis of 'so much of the Church Order and Discipline as the Episcopalian, Presbyterian, and Independent are agreed in': similar associations were formed in other counties, but after Cromwell's death, in Baxter's words, 'The poor Church of Christ, the sober, sound, religious part, was like Christ that was crucified between two malefactors—the prophane and formal Persecutors on one hand, and the fanatical dividing sectary on the other.'

At the Restoration his hopes revived: Charles made him his chaplain and offered him a bishopric: but the Savoy Conference, and the Cavalier Parliament, soon destroyed his hopes. He refused to accept the Act of Uniformity and was one of the ejected ministers, though he always regarded himself as a loyal member of the Church of England and even as late as 1670 was offered 'a College in the University or a Bishoprick'.

---

[1] But Baxter had no tolerance for Papists on the one hand or for Quakers on the other: his attitude towards the former lost him the sympathy of Charles II.

He was a voluminous writer and a great controversialist,[1] but 'what lay behind all his striving was an intense desire for Peace and Concord, in order to attain a state in which the Church should be able to see its duty clearly and to attend to it without distraction'.[2]

His most famous work was *The Saints' Everlasting Rest*, and his best-known hymn that which ends,

> My knowledge of that life is small,
> The eye of faith is dim,
> But 'tis enough that Christ knows all,
> And I shall be with Him.

JOHN BUNYAN (1628–88) owed his first interest in religion to his wife: some books which her father had left her when he died 'did beget within me some desires to Religion: so that, because I knew no better, I fell in very eagerly with the Religion of the times; to wit, to go to Church twice a day, . . . and there should very devoutly both say and sing as others did, yet retaining my wicked Life'.

But 'upon a day the good providence of God did cast me to Bedford . . . and in one of the Streets of the town, I came where there were three or four poor *Women* sitting at a door in the Sun, and talking about the things of God. . . . Their talk was about a new Birth, the work of God on their hearts'. He 'began to look into the Bible with new eyes'.

He passed through a long period of uncertainty, sometimes thinking he had sinned a sin against the Holy Ghost, and sometimes comforted by texts which flashed into his mind, till at last 'now did my Chains fall off my Legs indeed . . . now went I also home rejoicing, for the Grace and Love of God'. On the title page of his spiritual autobiography, *Grace Abounding*, he wrote, 'I have been vile myself, but have obtained mercy, and I would have my companions in sin partake of mercy too.'

He was received into the Baptist Church in 1653, and two years later, though the invitation to do so 'did much dash and abash' his spirit, he began to preach. He was threatened with imprisonment in 1658 under the Commonwealth, and in

[1] It is a melancholy fact that Baxter was sent to prison by Judge Jeffreys who cried, 'Thou hast written books enough to load a cart, and every book is full of sedition as an egg is full of meat'.

[2] F. J. Powicke, *Life of Richard Baxter*, p. 280.

1660 was put in gaol, where he remained with a brief interval till 1672, having been convicted by the local justices for 'an Upholder and Maintainer of Unlawful Assemblies and Conventicles, and for not conforming to the National Worship of the Church of England': during the later years of his imprisonment he was allowed to meet with his congregation, and in 1672 received a licence to preach and a pardon. In 1678 he was again imprisoned, though only for six months.

It was during this last imprisonment that he wrote the first part of the *Pilgrim's Progress*, followed by the *Holy War*, and by the second part six years later.

He was not a skilled theologian, and was at times both bitter and intolerant, but though his great book has been rightly called 'the prose epic of English Puritanism' it is far too great a book to belong to any party, and from the first it appealed to the hearts of all Christian people, as it has done ever since.

THE INDEPENDENTS were those who held that the whole past history of the Church was a vast mistake: the kingdom of God consisted of 'the worthiest, be they never so few': this was the doctrine of the 'Brownists' in Elizabeth's reign. Browne's motto was *Reformation without tarrying for any*, and his followers, recognizing Christ as their only governor, rejected all organization. His follower Barrow, who denied 'any laws for the Church other than Christ hath already left in his Word', was executed in 1593.

John Robinson led out to Leyden in 1608 a little flock which he had gathered round him in Norfolk, but they were not happy in Holland, for the other Protestants regarded them as religious anarchists, and in 1620 101 persons got leave to sail from England and set sail for America in the *Mayflower*, an event from which great results were to come.

The Long Parliament, which wished to establish the severe discipline of Presbyterianism, naturally did not approve of them, but under Cromwell they came into power, though he maintained the connexion of Church and State which they disapproved. They soon began to feel the need of some organization, saying that 'the generality of our Churches have been in a manner like so many ships (though holding forth the same general colours) launched singly, and sailing apart and alone in the Vast Ocean of these tumultuating times, and exposed to every wind of doctrine ... without so much as holding out common lights to others, whereby to know where we are.'

They survive in the Congregationalists, whose principle is that while Christian Churches should hold communion with each other 'no Church, or union of Churches, has any right or power to interfere with the faith or discipline of any other Church'—in other words, that the Church cannot exist as a visible united body.

THE QUAKERS,[1] who owe their origin to GEORGE FOX (1624–1691) were the most independent body of all, and have remained so ever since. Fox was apprenticed to a shoemaker in Leicestershire, who also employed him to tend sheep. As he grew up he became conscious of an 'inner light', and his message to every man was that he should be true to the light within him. 'Keep your feet on the top of the mountains and sound deep to the witness of God in every man' was his advice to his followers, who were at first called 'Children of the Light', though they soon came to call themselves 'Friends in Truth'.

Fox was repeatedly imprisoned, sometimes with shocking cruelty, and spent some six years in gaol, being sentenced for blasphemy under the Commonwealth. He did not claim to have a new Gospel but 'a new revelation of the good old Gospel', and declared that 'the Everlasting Gospel was being preached again by the same Holy Ghost as the Apostles were in, and received from Heaven as they received it'. He valued the Bible not so much in itself as because it confirmed what he learnt by direct revelation. 'He was prepared to *trust* the direct and personal experience of the Spirit's immediate presence and guidance to such an extent as to base his whole Church policy upon it', and therefore 'to sweep away all outward safeguards such as an ordained ministry, sacraments, set forms of worship and traditional creeds'.[2]

He joined with other 'seekers' in the north of England, and

The name Quaker is said to have been given by a justice whom Fox bade to tremble at the word of the Lord: others attribute it to the trembling and spiritual stress sometimes shown at Friends' meetings.

[2] Brayshaw, *The Quakers*, p. 57; Grubb, *What is Quakerism?*, p. 27.

in 1654 they sent out an organized mission whose members went by twos and threes throughout England and Wales. To one scholar who listened they seemed at first 'a poor, weak, silly, contemptible generation who had some smatterings of truth in them', but when later on he heard Fox himself preaching 'the mystery of the gospel of peace' he became a follower with his wife, and proved his loyalty by suffering six imprisonments. The early Quakers suffered much from mob-violence as well as from the law, for the crowds were annoyed at the sight of men and women sitting in silence—'mumming and dumming'—and pledged to non-resistance of injury.

They suffered severely under Charles II and James II as their numbers grew not only in England but in America, to which their doctrines had spread. In 1676 William Penn, a rich young man, who had been converted to Quakerism ten years before, became part owner of New Jersey, and in five years more than 1,400 Friends had made their way there: his attitude to the Indians was very different from that of others, for the Quakers gave a fair price for land, treated them well, and laboured for their conversion. Pennsylvania became the most consistently free and the most consistently prosperous of the colonies.

Quakers have no ordered form of worship, but allow men and women to utter prayers or to give any message committed to them, for 'all Friends everywhere in the living Spirit and living Power and in the heavenly light dwell'. They find silence quite as edifying as speech, in their effort to 'feel the power of God in one another' that all may be as one family building up one another and helping one another.

In the eighteenth century, when practical toleration had come, they became rather ineffective, seeming to pay less attention to their great principles than to matters of outward observance in dress and speech: as one of them said in 1800, 'We are just considered as a good sort of people in the main who refuse to fight and swear and pay tithes', but they played a noble part in helping to abolish the slave trade: they con-demned it as early as 1727, and in 1761 disowned all Friends concerned in it: in 1783 they formed the first society for its abolition. They began then to acquire that great reputation for brave and unselfish work for others which they have steadily maintained.

We shall naturally ask why it was that all these good Christian men found it so impossible to agree: the answer is that in the seventeenth century the idea of toleration in religious matters barely existed at all.[1]

To begin with, no one was prepared to tolerate Roman Catholicism. For this there were two reasons, the first, that the memory of Mary's persecutions still remained, while the conduct of Roman Catholic powers like Spain, and (in a less degree) France, suggested that they had no idea of tolerating Protestantism: secondly, the Roman cause was bound up with politics, and it was easy to maintain that no Roman Catholic could be a loyal subject of the English crown. This of course became a commonplace after James II's expulsion.

The Church of England had become disastrously dependent on the State and found the temptation to use the State's power too strong to resist. We may grant that its object, to recreate a united Church of England, was sound, and that it did in fact offer a middle course which appealed to most of the country, but its reliance on the State, and its alliance with the king, alienated a great many of the best Christians, and gave rise to the belief that it cared more for its position than for morality. The strength of the Puritans, as has been said, lay in their moral appeal.

The Puritans were quite as intolerant as the Church of England, and, though their best leaders, like Baxter, tried to restrain them, they refused to allow those who believed in government by bishops to practise their faith or to use their Prayer Book, and wantonly destroyed the contents of their churches.

The Independents might seem more likely to tolerate, but they were not in practice ready for toleration: we have seen that it was under Cromwell that the last Roman Catholic was put to death for his religion in England, and he showed no mercy to Papists in Ireland. Even the Independents of the

[1] The Quakers may seem to provide an exception, but they were by no means tolerant in practice of what they thought superstitious, and we must add that they never were tested by having the power to persecute.

Mayflower, who had crossed the sea for the sake of religious liberty, sent back to England those who preferred to use their Prayer Book, and Roger Williams, who first maintained absolute liberty of conscience, had to depart from Massachusetts to New Jersey.

It was an obscure Anglican who first put into shape the great argument on which tolerance rests: 'it were better that many false doctrines were published, especially with a good intention and not of weakness only, than that one truth should be forcibly smothered or wilfully concealed'.[1]

The fact is that every one was still aiming at an external unity which was at that time impossible unless on a basis wider than anyone was prepared to accept: to abandon all organization proved impossible even for the Independents. As so often happens, it was the extreme men on both sides, and by no means the most religious, who took control, and the results were unhappy for the cause of true religion.

XIII

THE BEGINNINGS OF TOLERATION

THE quarter of a century covered by the reigns of William and Anne (1689–1714) was definitely a time of religious progress. The Toleration Act of 1689 greatly improved the position of the Nonconformists and Queen Anne's real interest in religion was a boon to the Church.

It is true that it had suffered a great loss when many of its best leaders (such as Bishop Ken) had refused to take the oath of allegiance to King William. They had preached the doctrine of 'passive obedience' to the king, and having sworn loyalty to King James they were not prepared to change over like the famous 'Vicar of Bray'. They had been ready to resist James' illegal acts, and among them were five of the seven bishops who had opposed him: they were quite ready to suffer for their convictions but not ready to abandon them at the bidding of parliament.

[1] Creighton, *Historical Lectures*, p. 40.

It is easy to see how great was the loss when such men, followed by 400 of the best clergy, went into retirement under the name of 'Nonjurors'. They may have been mistaken but it is impossible not to respect them.[1]

But in spite of this great loss religion kept, or gained, a strong hold on ordinary English life: one evidence of this is the number of books of devotion written and sold about this time, of which a good example is *The Whole Duty of Man*, first published in 1657, which ran through countless editions and was read by dissenters as often as *The Pilgrim's Progress* was read by Anglicans.

At the end of the century there was a remarkable growth of moral and religious societies, of which two remain to this day. The Society for the Promotion of Christian Knowledge was founded in 1698 to support religious education in schools, to help the Church in the colonies, and to supply good literature at a cheap price, and these objects it still pursues. The Society for the Propagation of the Gospel in Foreign Parts, which grew out of it in 1701, was primarily concerned with British Colonies and has only gradually developed into a great missionary society.

Queen Anne, a really religious woman, promoted the building of churches and did much to alleviate the poverty of the clergy: Dean Swift gives the income of country incumbents at from £20 to £60 a year, while curates rarely received more than £30. It is extremely difficult to form an opinion of their social standing, but it may safely be said that it deteriorated in the half-century following the death of Queen Anne. Un-

---

[1] An 'Epitaph on Passive Obedience' shows their point of view and satirizes those who quickly abandoned their principles:

> In hope of sudden resurrection,
> Certain and sure beneath this stone
> Passive Obedience lies interred,
> By Church of England men averred:*
> She was not long since in great favour
> As any doctrine of our Saviour.
>
> .   .   .   .   .
>
> Beware and see how you contest
> With that supreme grace, Interest;
> For her great crime upon her trial
> Was anti-Christian self-denial.

> * averred = asserted.

written sermons were beginning to replace written discourses: an instance of the popularity of the latter is the strange fact that after Tillotson died in 1694 2,500 guineas were paid for the copyright of two volumes of his sermons. It was still customary to use the black gown in the pulpit, though the surplice was used in all other parts of the services: 'if he preach in a fool's coat, we will go and hear him' writes a Puritan in 1696 when he saw his first surplice in a pulpit.

Church music had become popular after the Restoration in spite of Puritan protests. One of them bitterly complained of the 'hideous noise of music, both of singers and instruments' at Durham, and declared that owing to the 'confusedness of voices, some squeaking, some bleating, some roaring and thundering, with a multitude of melodious instruments, shakbuts, and cornets and organs, the greatest part of the service is no better understood than if it were in Hebrew or Irish.'[1]

Purcell (1658–95) won the place of the greatest of English musicians.[2] Tate and Brady's metrical version of the Psalms was authorized by William III in 1696 and superseded the version of Sternhold and Hopkins,[3] but the common use of hymns was still in the future. Any one who will read the morning and evening hymns written by Bishop Ken the Nonjuror will see that their day was soon to come, and Christians of every type could join in such verses as:

[1] That sturdy Puritan, Andrew Fairservice, was equally contemptuous of 'the curate linking awa at it in his white sark', of the 'clauts' o' cauld parritch' he gave in his discourse, and of 'the musicians playing on whistles'. Scott, *Rob Roy*, Chap. xvii.

[2] His epitaph in Westminster Abbey, where he was organist, runs, 'Here lies Henry Purcell Esq., who left this Place, and is gone to that Blessed Place where only his Harmony can be exceeded.'

[3] In 1646 parliament had substituted the version of Mr. Rous whom Clarendon calls 'an old gentleman of Devonshire of very mean understanding'. The later change was not entirely for the better: for instance, in their version of Psalm xviii. 10, the older version ran:

> On cherubs and on cherubims
> Full royally he rode,
> And on the wings of mighty winds
> Came flying all abroad.

for which Tate and Brady substituted:

> The chariot of the Lord of Hosts,
> Which troops of active angels drew,
> Upon a tempest's mighty wings
> With most amazing swiftness flew.

Direct, control, suggest, this day
All I design, or do, or say,
That all my powers, with all their might,
In Thy sole glory may unite.

Any one who looks at our hymn-books will see how much
they owe to Isaac Watts (1674–1748): his most famous hymns
are 'When I survey the wondrous Cross' and 'Jesus shall
reign' and 'O God, our help in ages past'.

Attempts, not wholly unsuccessful, were made to secure
more frequent celebrations of the Holy Communion, which had
been discouraged by the Puritans when in power: even the rule,
made before the Civil War, that there should be celebrations
on the first Sunday of every month, 'or at least thrice in the
year', had been laxly observed. Weekly communions now
became the rule at Canterbury, York, Durham, Gloucester,
and St. Paul's: they had always been kept at Ely and Worcester: and they became common in parish churches in
London. The rule of daily morning and evening prayer was
also more generally observed. 'Charity schools' in which the
children of the poor were clothed and fed, as well as educated,
were founded by the Church: their numbers are shown by the
fact that 4,000 such children were assembled to welcome
George I on his accession in 1714.

It is presumably one of the teachers in these 'Charity
Schools' whom Goldsmith describes so charmingly in the
Deserted Village, who kept his children in such good order,
and whose learning amazed his neighbours:

The village all declared how much he knew;
'Twas certain he could write and cipher too;
Lands he could measure, terms and tides presage,
And even the story ran that he could gauge.
In arguing, too, the parson own'd his skill,
For, even though vanquish'd, he could argue still;
While words of learned length and thundering sound
Amazed the gazing rustics ranged around;
And still they gazed, and still the wonder grew,
That one small head could carry all he knew.

Altogether this brief period marks a general revival of
Church life, which unfortunately did not long survive the

chilling atmosphere of the eighteenth century, when the close connexion of the Church with the government was again to prove disastrous.

Addison, in his picture of Sir Roger de Coverley at church, gives a charming picture of the Christian country squire at the end of this period.

My friend Sir Roger, being a good churchman, has beautified the inside of his church with several texts of his own chusing: he has likewise given a handsome pulpit-cloth, and railed in the communion-table at his own expence. He has often told me, that at his coming to his estate he found his parishioners very irregular; and that, in order to make them kneel and join in the responses, he gave every one of them a hassock and a common-prayer-book; and at the same time employed an itinerant singing-master, who goes about the country for that purpose, to instruct them rightly in the tunes of the psalms; upon which they now very much value themselves, and indeed out-do most of the country churches that I have ever heard.

As Sir Roger is landlord to the whole congregation, he keeps them in very good order, and will suffer no body to sleep in it besides himself; for, if by chance he has been surprised into a short nap at sermon, upon recovering out of it he stands up and looks about him, and if he sees any body else nodding, either wakes them himself, or sends his servants to them.

XIV

THE INFLUENCE OF WESLEY

It is generally agreed that for more than half the century religion in England was at a very low ebb: the reasons for this are easy to see.

(1) The disputes of the century before, and the wrongs done on both sides, had left those who cared for Christianity hopelessly divided. The Roman Catholics were generally regarded as bad citizens, and so long as there was a prospect of the restoration of a Roman Catholic king (i.e., at least till 1745)

the government could not be blamed for taking that view.[1] The Church of England still suffered from that close association with the government which had begun with Charles I and Laud: there was an excuse for this so long as the king and his ministers really cared for religion (as Charles I, with all his faults, unquestionably did) but in the first half of the eighteenth century Queen Anne was the only sovereign of whom that could be said,[2] and the ministry only cared for the Church as a useful political ally. The result was that the Church became increasingly worldly, and much more concerned with its own rights and properties than with the preaching of the Gospel.

The Nonconformists gained in credit by comparison, for they had no rights or properties to encourage selfishness, and it is always good for a religious body to be persecuted, but the laws against them, though not rigorously enforced, naturally lessened their influence.

(2) The eighteenth century was an 'age of Reason'. In its early years a great deal of very valuable work was done (as by Bishop Butler, Bishop Berkeley, and William Law) to show the 'reasonableness' of Christianity, and to put it on a firm intellectual basis.

But, though the Christian religion *is* reasonable, that is not its chief characteristic: it would never occur to any one to say how 'reasonable' Christ was, or to call the Gospels 'reasonable'. The eighteenth century distrusted enthusiasm of all kinds, and the sense of proportion which makes its architecture or its furniture so attractive tends to encourage mere respectability in conduct. It has been said that eighteenth-century poets call for fire from heaven but in such decorous language that no one thinks of looking for the extinguisher, and the famous remark of Bishop Butler to John Wesley is very characteristic of the century: 'Sir, the pretending to

[1] All High Churchmen tended to be regarded as Jacobites, as indeed some of them were. (A High Churchman is one who has a 'high' view of the Church, just as a man may have a 'high' view of the rights and powers of a king or of parliament.)

[2] Anne's plan for building 52 churches in London was dropped by Walpole when only some 14 had been built.

extraordinary revelation and gifts of the Holy Ghost is a horrid thing, a very horrid thing.'

In these circumstances it is not surprising that religion ceased to make much appeal. Though the Churchmen were remarkably, and wisely, wide awake in defending the faith in argument, the sleepy time had set in. Convocation, the Church's parliament, ceased to meet in 1717, and did not reassemble for 135 years: many clergy were content with reading their services and preaching on Sundays, and they lost the moral influence they had once had as their general credit declined. No doubt there were bright exceptions: Goldsmith in his *Deserted Village*, published in 1770, certainly exaggerates the merits of the 'good old times' for the sake of contrast, but his picture of the village parson cannot be entirely the work of imagination:

> A man he was to all the country dear,
> And passing rich with forty pounds a year;
> Remote from towns he ran his godly race,
> Nor e'er had chang'd, nor wished to change, his place,
>
> .   .   .   .   .   .
>
> More skill'd to raise the wretched than to rise.
> His house was known to all the vagrant train,
> He chid their wand'rings but reliev'd their pain;
>
> .   .   .   .   .   .
>
> Careless their merits, or their faults to scan,
> His pity gave ere charity began.

He may not have been an eloquent preacher but such was the affection which he won that truth 'from his lips prevailed with double sway And fools, who came to scoff, remained to pray'. We cannot tell how many there were like him, in the first half of the eighteenth century, who by their piety and their good deeds 'Allured to brighter worlds, and led the way.'

A few years later (1783) Crabbe in *The Village* draws a very different picture of the village priest:

> A jovial youth, who thinks his Sunday's task
> As much as God or man can fairly ask;
> The rest he gives to loves and labours light,
> To fields the morning and to feasts the night.

There were other reasons for the weakness of the Church. English people generally were equally afraid of a return to Romanism—'the Pretender, the Mass and wooden shoes'— and of a return to Puritanism, so that two sections of society, both of which were full of religious zeal, were equally suspected. Again, in the Church itself, there was a division between the 'inferior clergy' most of whom were Jacobites at heart, and the bishops who, as they owed their appointment to the Court, were bound to be supporters of King George. The Nonjurors, who, as has been said, numbered among them some of the best of the clergy, naturally disapproved of the House of Hanover even more than of Queen Anne, and their loss was a great source of weakness.

But it was a Nonjuror, WILLIAM LAW, whose writings were responsible for the religious revival which may be said to have begun with the 'conversion' of John Wesley in 1738. Law's *Serious Call to a Devout and Holy Life*, of which more will be said later, was published in 1728, and that and his *Treatise on Christian Perfection* had much to do both with the Methodist movement, which ultimately parted from the Church, and with the Evangelical revival within it.

The Methodist movement began with a small society formed at Oxford in 1729 by CHARLES WESLEY, and the nickname of Methodist was given them 'because of their strict conformity to the method of study prescribed by the statutes of the University.' JOHN WESLEY joined them, and by 1733 they numbered fifteen. They were all orthodox in every point: they met almost every evening, 'reading the scriptures and provoking one another to love and to good works'; they began visiting the prisoners in gaol and the sick.

In 1735 John and Charles Wesley sailed as missionaries to Georgia, a colony which had just been established by General Oglethorpe. John had hoped that he would be able to preach the Gospel to the Indians, and was disappointed when he found that he was little more than a parish priest to the colonists: he returned to England in 1738. On the voyage out an event occurred which had a great effect on him. The ship was caught in a storm, and all were much alarmed, passengers and crew alike, except some German Christians of a sect called

Moravians. Wesley asked one of them whether their women and children were not afraid: 'he replied mildly, "No, our women and children are not afraid to die."'[1]

But he says himself, 'I, who went to America to convert others, was never myself converted to God' till on 24 May 1738 'at a quarter before nine o'clock' he was converted as, at a meeting of a religious society in Aldersgate Street, he heard 'a person read Luther's Preface to the Epistle to the Romans, which teaches what justifying faith is. I felt my heart strangely warmed. I felt I did trust in Christ, Christ alone, for salvation; and an assurance was given me that He had taken away my sins, even mine, and then I testified openly to all there what I now first felt in my heart.'

So began a ministry which lasted till his death in 1791, in the course of which he is said to have travelled 250,000 miles, in days when travelling was slow, difficult, and dangerous, and to have preached 40,000 sermons. At the age of 80 he attributed his health and vigour, '(1) to the power of God, fitting me for what He calls me to. (2) To my still travelling four or five thousand miles a year. (3) To my still sleeping, night or day, whenever I want it. (4) To my rising at a set hour. (5) To my constant preaching, particularly in the morning.'

The reasons why the movement which he began ultimately separated from the Church are easy to understand, though it should be remembered that he himself remained, in his own opinion, a loyal Churchman to the end: two years before his death he preached to his followers saying,

Ye are a new phenomenon in the earth, a body of people who, being of no sect or party, are friends to all parties, and endeavour to forward all in heart-religion, in the knowledge and love of God and man. Ye yourselves were at first called in the Church of England; and though ye have and will have a thousand temptations to leave it, and set up for yourselves, regard them not; be Church of England men still; do not cast away the peculiar glory which God hath put upon you, and frustrate the design of Providence, the very end for which God hath raised you up.

---

[1] The Moravians also taught him the value of hymn-singing, which was to play so large a part in his later ministry.

But the methods which he adopted were not likely to be approved by the Church authorities of the time. It is a great mistake to suppose that all the bishops were indifferent to religion: many of them (especially those appointed by the influence of Queen Caroline) were good and learned men: one (Bishop Wilson of Sodor and Man) has real claims to saintliness: Wesley himself says that he received no blame from 'any of these venerable men. Only Archbishop Potter once said, "Those gentlemen are irregular; but they have done good, and I pray God to bless them." '

But 'irregularity' was precisely what shocked the eighteenth-century mind with its love for proportion and propriety, and it cannot be denied that Wesley's proceedings were irregular in the extreme. Like the friars of old, he invaded parishes with no respect for the wishes of the parish priest, and not all of them by any means welcomed the intrusion.

Many of those who objected did so simply because it *was* an intrusion, and because they did not wish to be disturbed in their idleness, but there were other and stronger grounds for objection. Wesley's preaching led to physical results which he records with satisfaction: 'some sank down, and there remained no strength in them: others exceedingly trembled and quaked. Some were torn with a kind of convulsive motion in every part of their bodies, and that so violently that often four or five persons could not hold one of them.' Or again, 'while I was speaking, one before me dropped down as dead, and presently a second and a third. Five others sank down in half an hour, most of whom were in violent agonies.' Even those who admired Wesley and sympathized with him did not share his satisfaction at this kind of testimony, and we cannot be surprised that ordinary respectable eighteenth-century Christians were definitely shocked by it.

It was clearly a case where the authorities of the Church should have met to discuss what should be done and have taken joint action: if they had done so, it would probably have been possible, as they were not really unsympathetic and Wesley was unquestionably loyal, to keep the movement within the Church, but no such discussion took place, and Convocation, as we have seen, had ceased to meet. The result

was that, towards the end of his life (in 1784), Wesley, who
had previously been content with commissioning lay preachers,
took the definite step of 'ordaining' ministers for Scotland
and America,[1] which made a schism inevitable, as ordination,
by the laws of the Church of England, could only be admin-
istered by a bishop.[2]

It is easy to believe that he took the step from 'a firm
desire to promote the glory of God and the spiritual welfare
of man', for those were the only objects he cared for, but at
the same time it was in direct contradiction to his own principles and made separation from the Church inevitable.

GEORGE WHITEFIELD, one of the original fifteen Oxford
Methodists, was, like Wesley, a clergyman of the Church of
England, but, unlike him, felt no loyalty to it: as he says
himself, in his early days he 'thought he had never well closed
a sermon without a lash at the fat downy doctors of the
Establishment'. His special contribution to the movement lay
in the introduction of open-air preaching, for which his marvellous voice (he could be clearly heard by 30,000 people) was
admirably fitted. Wesley at first disliked the idea, 'having
been all my life so tenacious of every point relating to decency
and order, that I should have thought the saving of souls
almost a sin if it had not been done in a church.' He and his
brother Charles tried for divine guidance on the matter by
opening their Bibles at random in search for texts, and when
this method failed, cast lots. The lot was favourable, and
open-air preaching became a striking feature of the movement.

Whitefield, who is said to have preached ten times a week
for 34 years, must have been an amazing orator; his gestures
were faultless: his voice sweet and musical: Garrick said he
could pronounce the word 'Mesopotamia' in such a way as
to move an audience to tears. His language was always
dramatic, often exaggerated, and not seldom in bad taste, but
he made all his hearers feel the infinite importance of his

[1] The shortage of ministers in America was due largely to the fact that it
was necessary for them to come home for ordination as there was no bishop
there. The Church had been trying for 30 years to get an American bishop
consecrated but the Nonconformists had protested, and the scheme was
dropped. One was finally consecrated in 1784 by Scotch bishops.
[2] See p. 131.

subject: he preached 'as a dying man to dying men', and was not afraid to dwell upon the terrors of hell, from which salvation was freely offered by Christ alone.

He appealed, with great success, to the emotions[1]—and this was a great achievement in the eighteenth century—but he could not, like Wesley, who had the qualities of a scholar and a statesman, appeal to the reason as well. He was a strong Calvinist, which led to a severance between him and Wesley, who held to the doctrine of free will.[2]

He became a chaplain of the Countess of Huntingdon, a rich Evangelical lady (and like him a Calvinist), whose sole object in life was to bring about a revival of religion in the upper classes. For this purpose she spent £100,000 in building or buying chapels in which she appointed ministers at her own pleasure. George III once said, 'I wish there was a Lady Huntingdon in every diocese in the kingdom', but her claim to appoint and dismiss chaplains was clearly 'irregular' and against her will she became a dissenter.[3]

The early Methodist preachers were exposed to abuse from

[1] Here is an example of his oratory: "The attendant angel is just about to leave the threshold of this sanctuary and ascend to heaven, and shall he ascend and not bear with him the news of one sinner among all this multitude reclaimed from the error of his way?' To give the greater effect to this exclamation Whitefield stamped with his foot, lifted up his hands and eyes to heaven, and cried aloud, 'Stop, Gabriel, stop ere you enter the sacred portals, and yet carry with you the news of one sinner converted to God!'

[2] The correspondence between them has been wittily summed up thus: 'Dear George, I have read what you have written on the subject of predestination, and God has taught me to see that you are wrong and that I am right. Yours affectionately, J. Wesley.' 'Dear John, I have read what you have written on the subject of predestination, and God has taught me that I am right and you are wrong. Yours affectionately, G. Whitefield.' Other Calvinists were by no means so courteous. Rowland Hill, for instance, called Wesley 'a gray-headed enemy of all righteousness', while Toplady (the author of 'Rock of Ages') said he was a low and puny tadpole in divinity 'actuated by Satanic shamelessness and Satanic guilt'. The Wesleyans, to their credit, did not reply in the same style.

[3] Two comments made by members of her congregation are very characteristic of the time. Bolingbroke told Whitefield that 'he had done great justice to the divine attributes in his discourse': the Duchess of Buckingham wrote, 'His doctrines are most repulsive. It is monstrous to be told that you have a heart as sinful as the common creatures that crawl the earth. This is highly offensive and insulting, and I cannot but wonder that your ladyship should relish any sentiments so much at variance with high rank and good breeding.'

every side: some, like Horace Walpole, absurdly accused them of being Papists in disguise, while others attacked them as Puritans who wished to rob life of its pleasures.[1] They were often threatened with violence and their lives were sometimes in danger, but nothing could quench their enthusiasm. It is difficult to exaggerate the good which they did in England, Ireland, and Wales in recalling men and women to a personal interest in religion.[2]

They can fairly be criticized for being too ready to frighten people into religion, for encouraging an excitement which was not far from madness, and a belief in witchcraft and in direct divine interference which could easily become superstitions. We have seen Wesley opening the Bible at random for guidance and settling important matters by lot, and though he himself had a real interest in history and criticism most of his followers tended to despise what they called 'human science'. But when full allowance has been made for such weaknesses, the debt of all English Christians to them is incalculable. One claim which Wesley made for his followers was abundantly justified: 'the world may not like our Methodist and Evangelical people, but the world cannot deny that they die well'.

In Wesleyan missionary work the pioneer was DR. COKE, a man of amazing energy (1747–1814). He was mayor of Brecon and a clergyman of the Church of England before he became a Methodist: but he responded to the call addressed to him by Wesley in 1776, 'Brother, go out, go out and preach the Gospel to all the world!' He planned a missionary society, and wished to attack India, but the East India Company still vetoed missions: he made attempts in West Africa, though without great success, and after the American war in 1784 was sent by Wesley to organize the Methodist societies of the United States.

This was the occasion of Wesley's break with the Church of England. He did not 'ordain' Coke, who was already a

[1] Wesley had a sentimental affection for Mary, Queen of Scots, which illogically led to the further accusation that his followers were not only disguised Papists but disguised Jacobites.
[2] 'Among its other effects, Methodism helped to save the middle and lower classes from sympathizing with the anti-Christian principles of the French revolution.' Lecky, *History of England in the Eighteenth Century*, iii, p. 146.

clergyman, but empowered him to ordain and consecrate a general superintendent or bishop in the United States, so founding the Methodist Episcopal Church of America. His action was severely blamed by his brother Charles.

Coke crossed the Atlantic 18 times, making five visits to the West Indies, where he established missions in all the principal islands. He was lavish of his own money, and found it hard to tolerate the prudence of the Committee (formed in 1793), which tried to keep his schemes within the limits of its resources.

His end was characteristically heroic: in 1813 the East India Company was induced to allow missionaries to go to India, and Coke, though now over 65, resolved to lead an expedition to Ceylon. The Methodist Conference was very doubtful, both because of his age and of the unknown expense involved. He offered to bear the whole expense himself and set out in December with six volunteers: on 3 May he died at sea. It is mainly due to him that the Wesleyans hold so honourable a place in the history of Christian missions.

The movement, which, as we have seen, began within the Church of England, naturally had a great effect upon it. Until Wesley first authorized lay preachers to administer the Communion (in 1760), there was nothing to prevent the most 'regular' clergy from imitating his methods, and some did so with great success—the so-called Evangelicals.

The most attractive of them was FLETCHER of Madeley, whom Voltaire chose when asked to name a character as perfect as that of our Lord, and whom another who knew him describes as 'an angel in human flesh': Wesley chose for the text for his funeral sermon, 'Mark the perfect man . . . for the end of that man is peace'. A slight illustration will show his power of uniting the simple things of life with the greatest: he told his cook 'to stir up the fire of divine love in her soul', and his housemaid 'to sweep every corner of her heart'. He excelled, as might be expected, in his dealings with children.

Another, very different, man was GRIMSHAW of Haworth who, like Wesley, had no scruple in invading other men's parishes. In his own parish he raised the number of communicants from 12 to nearly 1,200, and secured the proper observance of Sunday, sometimes, it was said, driving his parishioners to church with a horsewhip. His zeal (he sometimes preached 30 times a week), and his humility had a great effect. When he died, of a fever caught in visiting the sick, he cried, 'Here goes an unprofitable servant'.

There were other parish clergy of this kind, but it was not till after the accession of George III in 1760 that the Evangelical movement became really strong, and the 20 years before that represent the lowest depth to which the Church of England has ever sunk in energy and efficiency.

XV

TWO GREAT CHRISTIANS

BEFORE we deal with the period which begins in 1760 let us look at two great Christians of the earlier period.

WILLIAM LAW (1686–1761) can best be represented by some extracts from his books, and particularly the *Serious Call to a Devout and Holy Life*, which should be read by every one who cares either for religion or for literature: his purpose is to show that religion, if taken seriously, is the source of all goodness and all happiness. The reason, he says, why most people do not realize this is that they 'have not so much as the intention to please God in all their actions as the happiest and best thing in the world . . . Let a tradesman but have this intention, and it will make him a saint in his shop.'

There are some delightful pictures of half-hearted Christians. Calidus, the merchant, whose 'prayers are a short *ejaculation* or two, which he never misses in *stormy*, *tempestuous* weather, because he has always something or other at sea': Mundanus, who, as an old man, 'prays still in that little form of words which his mother used to hear him repeat night and morning when he was only six years of age': Negotius, whose one object is 'to grow continually richer and richer, and to raise an immense fortune before he dies': Flatus, whose soul is given to hunting, who 'leaped more *hedges* and *ditches* than had ever been known in so short a time, and always spoke to his dogs in great propriety of language.'

The portrait of Flavia is perhaps the best example of his method.

She is very *orthodox*, she talks warmly against *heretics* and *schismatics*, is generally at *Church* and often at the sacrament . . . If anyone asks Flavia to do something in charity, if she likes the person who makes the proposal, or happens to be in a right temper, she will toss him *half a crown* or a *crown* and tell him, if he knew what a *long Milliner's bill* she had just received, he would think it a great deal for her to give: but she is very positive that all *poor* people are *cheats* and *liars*. She would be a miracle of piety if she were but half so careful of her soul as she is of her body. . . .

If you visit Flavia on the Sunday, you will always meet good company . . . if you would know who is *rude* and *illnatured*, who is *vain* and *foppish*, who lives too *high*, and who is in *debt* . . . if you would know how cross Lucius is to his wife, what *illnatured* things he says to her when *nobody* hears him: if you would know how they hate one another in their *hearts*, though they appear so kind in public, you must visit Flavia on the *Sunday*.

I shall not take it upon me to say that it is impossible for Flavia to be saved: but this much must be said, that she has no grounds from Scripture to think she is in the way of salvation. She may as well say that she has every day *washed the saints' feet*, as that she has lived in Christian *humility* and *poverty of spirit*; and as reasonably think that she has taught a *Charity-school* as that she has lived in *works of charity*. She has as much reason to think that she has been a *sentinel* in an army, as that she has lived in *watching* and *self denial*, and it may as fairly be said that she lived by the labour of her hands, as that she had *given all diligence to make her calling and election sure*.

What a true Christian needs, he says elsewhere, is the spirit of love: where it is present 'all wants are satisfied, all Disorders of Nature are removed, no life is any longer a Burden, every Day is a Day of Peace'.

To those who 'live in a state of Half-piety, their religion is mere Yoke and Burden', but the man with a 'wise Ambition of all that Glory which God hath called him to, knows that the Happiness of the Heart is secure and safe to you against all Accidents. Here no Chances and Misfortunes can prevent your success, neither the Treachery of Friends nor the Malice of Enemies can disappoint you, it is only your own false

Heart that can rob you of this Happiness. . . . Do you but sincerely labour in the Lord, and then neither Height nor Depth, neither Life nor Death, neither Men nor Devils, can make your labour in vain'.

Lest it should be thought that all bishops in the early eighteenth century were idle and ineffective, let us glance at the career of THOMAS WILSON (1663–1755), bishop of Sodor and Man for 57 years.

He took great pains with his ordination candidates, who resided with him for a year before ordination: he paid constant surprise visits to his clergy to keep them up to the mark: he instituted parochial schools throughout his diocese and parish libraries. He wrote religious books in Manx for the benefit of the people, and started a Manx translation of the Bible: he was for some time the only physician on the island, and when others came resigned to them all patients who were able to pay, continuing to minister to the rest; his 'poor chest' (though his own income was only £300 a year) provided corn for the poor and spectacles for the blind.[1]

He restored in the island the primitive Church discipline, and sinners were excluded from Communion and punished in other ways. A slanderer was compelled publicly to lay his finger on his mouth saying, 'Tongue, thou hast lied' before all the congregation: clergy and laity alike were kept in strict control. When a new governor came who resented his action and imprisoned him for refusing to pay a fine, it was only Wilson's intercession which saved the governor's house from destruction: the people crowded round the prison while he preached through the bars. He was several times offered other bishoprics but he refused saying, 'No, an't please your Majesty, I will not leave my wife in my old age because she is poor.'

No doubt a small diocese like his was comparatively easy to administer and his discipline might have been hard to carry out elsewhere, but his zeal and unselfishness were an inspiration to all who knew him.

[1] He was helped by Lady Betty Hastings, to whom Steele paid what Thackeray called 'the finest compliment ever paid to a lady' when he said, 'To love her is a liberal education'.

XVI

A RELIGIOUS REVIVAL, FROM 1760–1800

THE last forty years of the century showed a considerable
advance in religious affairs and in particular a greater attention
to what may be called 'practical' Christianity. In its earlier
years the Church had been attending to the intellectual
defence of religion (and had met with considerable success),
while the Methodists were at first mainly concerned with the
saving of individual souls, in which, as we have seen, they had
also been very successful. But there had been little attempt,
except in particular cases, to bring Christianity to bear on
social questions. The fact that the Court, for the first time
for half a century, was morally respectable had its effect in
calling attention to moral problems. Philanthropy—a good
eighteenth-century word—became definitely associated with
religion through the influence of the Evangelicals.

That influence was greatly strengthened by WILLIAM
COWPER (1731–1800), who became the most popular poet of
his day; the author of *John Gilpin* wrote several famous
hymns, and the bulk of his work is devoted to preaching
Christianity as the Evangelical party saw it. His own 'conversion' is described in some famous lines:

> I was a stricken deer that left the herd
> Long since; with many an arrow deep infixed
> My panting side was charged, when I withdrew
> To seek a tranquil death in distant shades.
> There was I found by One who had Himself
> Been hurt by the archers. In His side He bore,
> And in His hands and feet, the cruel scars.

He was full of criticism of the idle priests who neglected
their duties, and full of praise for philanthropists like John
Howard, the reformer of prisons, and rich men like Thornton
who

> make gain a fountain, whence proceeds
> A stream of liberal and heroic deeds.

We find in him one of the earliest protests against the slave traders—the

> merchants rich in cargoes of despair,
> Who drive a loathsome traffic, gauge and span
> And buy the muscles and the bones of man.

His works, as we can see from Jane Austen, had a great influence on the rising generation.

Cowper was much influenced by that extraordinary man JOHN NEWTON (1725–1807) whose career is almost incredible. He went to sea at 11 years old, became a midshipman, deserted, was recaptured, and reduced to a common seaman; he exchanged into a slave ship and suffered every sort of ill-treatment from the slave-dealer and his negro mistress. He taught himself geometry, drawing Euclid's diagrams on the sand: he taught himself Latin with a Horace and a Latin Bible. 'His conversion was brought about by the combined influences of Thomas à Kempis, of a very narrow escape from shipwreck, of the impression made by the sights of the mighty deep, and of the disregarded but not forgotten teachings of his pious mother.'[1] He became captain of a slave ship and made several voyages without, it seems, any idea of its iniquity: he says he 'never knew sweeter or more fragrant hours of divine communion' than on his last two voyages to Guinea. But he disliked being a gaoler, and asked Providence to find him a more humane calling: his prayer was answered by a fit of apoplexy which unfitted him for life at sea: he settled in Liverpool as a custom house officer, and became a disciple of Whitefield and a friend of Wesley.

He decided to seek ordination, but it was five years before he could find a bishop to ordain him: at last in 1764 the bishop of Lincoln agreed to do so, and he secured the curacy of Olney,[2] where he became the friend and guide of Cowper. This was not without its dangers, for his Calvinism, though not of a violent kind, encouraged the poet's tendency to melancholy

---

[1] Goldwin Smith, *Cowper* ('English Men of Letters Series'), p. 38.
[2] Lord Dartmouth, who gave him the living, is described by Cowper as
> One who wears a coronet and prays,
which suggests that piety was uncommon in the higher ranks of society.

madness:[1] still his happiest years were spent while ministering
to the poor under Newton's direction. In 1780 he moved to
London and for 27 years was the spiritual adviser of most of
the lay Evangelicals. He wrote many hymns, of which the
best known are 'Glorious things of thee are spoken' and 'How
sweet the Name of Jesus sounds', but perhaps his best verse
is from another hymn:

> Thou art coming to a King,
> Large petitions with thee bring;
> For His grace and power are such
> None can ever ask too much.

In his old age, a friend urged him to stop his preaching before
he broke down: 'I cannot stop', he said, raising his voice,
'What! shall the old African blasphemer stop while he can
speak?'

Among the debts which we owe to the Evangelicals is the
reform of the prison system: JOHN HOWARD (1726–90) in 1773
became High Sheriff of Bedfordshire, and was shocked to find
that prisoners, even when acquitted, were often kept in gaol
till they had paid various fees to the gaoler: he suggested that
the gaoler should be paid a fixed salary, and when he was told
that there was no precedent for it, he rode out into the neighbouring counties to try to find one. In his first two months
he found that at Northampton felons were kept in damp cells
11 feet below ground with no straw to lie on: at Winchester
(the same depth below ground) 20 prisoners had died of gaol
fever in a year. At Gloucester criminals of every age, sex,
and character were kept together in one room with no court-
yard in which to walk, while at Nottingham you had to go
down 37 steps into the dungeon.

These discoveries whetted his interest, and for the remaining 17 years of his life he never ceased visiting prisons and
bombarding all authorities with demands for reform. He
travelled all over Europe seeking, as Cowper says of him,

---

[1] That his Calvinism was not extreme is shown by his repeating with
gusto the saying of an old woman of Olney about predestination: 'Ah, I have
settled that point; for if God had not chosen me before I was born, I am
sure He would have seen nothing to have chosen me for afterwards.'

Not the proud monuments of Greece and Rome,
But knowledge such as only dungeons teach
And only sympathy like thine could reach.

These travels of more than 50,000 miles cost him some
£30,000: the gaol fever was so common and so dangerous that
in many prisons the authorities would not accompany him:
he found that, on the whole, England in the treatment of
criminals was shamefully below the average of the Continent.
'Nowhere else were the executions so numerous. Nowhere
else were they conducted with such revolting indecency, and
in scarcely any other country were the abuses in prisons so
gross, so general and so demoralizing.'[1]

When he died, in Russia, of fever caught while inspecting
military prisons there, he had amply earned the epitaph
written by his friend Mr. Whitbread for his monument in
St. Paul's, 'He trod an open, but unfrequented, path to
immortality.'

Another subject to which they gave attention was that of
religious education.

HANNAH MORE (1745–1833), a friend of Dr. Johnson and
Garrick, and a disciple of Newton, wrote after her conversion
a book called *Thoughts on the Importance of the Manners of
the Great to General Society*, attacking card-playing and
gambling and urging the better observance of Sunday, followed by a series of Tracts, of which two million were sold in
the first year. She was so struck by the spiritual destitution
of Cheddar (in which only one Bible could be found and that
used to prop a flowerpot) that she decided to establish schools
for the education of poor children, which began in 1789, being
financed by Wilberforce and Thornton, and spread over ten
parishes. Next year they undertook adult education, dealing
not only with religion but with the teaching of useful handi-
crafts: by the end of the century they had greatly improved
conditions in that diocese.

Catechizing on Sunday, though enjoined by the bishops,
and carried out by some of the clergy, was by no means
common. ROBERT RAIKES (1735–1811), the proprietor of a

---

[1] Lecky, *History of England in the Eighteenth Century*, vii, p. 331

Gloucester newspaper, and Mr. Stock his rector, started four Sunday schools there in 1780 and the scheme soon spread throughout England. The Methodists took up the idea, John Wesley blessed it, and Queen Charlotte helped to establish them in Windsor. Before the end of the century there were Sunday schools in almost every well-managed parish in England: in many cases they supplied in those days the whole of a child's education, and reading, writing, and arithmetic were taught as well as religious knowledge, and the child might be in school for four or five hours a day.

It was religion which had inspired in Alfred's day the first attempts at education, and the monasteries which had provided the early teaching of the Middle Ages, so it was fitting that the first efforts at some system of teaching for poor children should have a Christian origin.

But far the greatest philanthropic work which we owe to the Evangelicals was the abolition of slavery[1] in British dominions and of the slave-trade. It was WILLIAM WILBER-FORCE and 'the Clapham sect' (a company of rich and pious Evangelicals who worshipped under Henry Venn at Clapham church) who carried the movement to its triumphant end— the abolition of the slave-trade in 1807, and the abolition of slavery throughout the Empire in 1833 at a cost of 20 million pounds to the mother country.

The title of 'father' of the movement is rightly given to GRANVILLE SHARP, who in 1772 secured, after seven years' struggle, the famous decision of Lord Mansfield that the power to enforce slavery never was in use in England nor acknowledged by the law. The last words of his judgement were, 'The state of slavery is so odious that nothing can be suffered to support it but positive law: whatever inconveniences therefore may follow from the decision . . . the black must be discharged.'

The 'inconveniences' were great, for there were then some 14,000 slaves in England, but the 'inconveniences' of

---

[1] Though it should not be forgotten that the Quakers had been the first to protest against the slave-trade, and formed a society for its abolition in 1783.

abolishing the slave-trade were far greater: before it was finally stopped it was estimated that the number of negroes conveyed in British ships was 57,000 a year. The West Indian traders maintained that their existence depended on the trade.

Wilberforce, who was 'converted' in 1785, soon brought the matter before the House of Commons: he was member for Yorkshire, and had succeeded by his amazing enthusiasm and eloquence in convincing his constituents that the slave-trade was iniquitous. He was a friend of Pitt, who sympathized with his cause, and when he first brought it before parliament its prospects seemed bright. He could tell his hearers of the horrors of the 'Middle Passage', and could prove to them that of every hundred negroes carried from Africa not more than fifty lived to work in the islands.

But the West Indian opposition, and that of Liverpool, one of the chief slave ports, was very strong, and the outbreak of the French Revolution (which had been followed by a rising of emancipated slaves in St. Domingo) and, later on, our war with France, occupied the public mind. In spite of Pitt's support, a motion for immediate abolition was rejected in 1792, and it was not till after Pitt's death that it was passed in 1807. It is a remarkable and creditable fact that it was carried in the middle of a great war at a time when no other agitation for any reform was allowed. It is interesting to notice that it had been a great Christian bishop, Wulfstan of Worcester, who had successfully protested against a similar trade more than eight centuries before.[1]

The Evangelicals continued their struggle, and Wilberforce lived just long enough to hear that slavery had been entirely abolished in the Empire: another great Evangelical, Fowell Buxton, had succeeded to the leadership of the cause.

The other great achievement of the Evangelicals was the arousing of an interest in foreign missions. It is hardly an exaggeration to say that since the Reformation no one had ever been sent out from this country to preach the Gospel to the heathen: the S.P.G. was mainly concerned with British

[1] See p. 50.

subjects abroad, and, as we have seen, John Wesley had found that he was not expected to minister to the Indians.[1]

The first English missionary in the modern sense was WILLIAM CAREY (1761–1834), a Baptist cobbler, perhaps the strangest cobbler who ever lived. He taught himself Latin and Greek, he picked up Italian in his spare time, he got a minister to teach him Hebrew that he might read the Psalms in the original language, and he made a start on Dutch and French, always working at his shoes with books before him. He started preaching in 1782, walking 12 miles every Sunday for the purpose, and by 1787 was a regular Baptist minister with a salary of £10 a year, and seven shillings and sixpence a week which he got from a night school.

Happening to read Captain Cook's journal, he said to himself, 'Those South Sea Islanders need the Gospel', and at a ministers' meeting in Northampton raised the question whether the command to the Apostles to preach to all nations did not apply to all succeeding ministers. The president made the famous answer, 'Young man, sit down! When God pleases to convert the heathen, He will do it without your aid or mine.'

But Carey was not satisfied, and a missionary society was formed with an original income of £13 2s. 6d. He offered to go, though his wife refused to accompany him: but enough money was raised to take Carey and a naval surgeon called Thomas to India. But the East India Company refused a licence to a missionary: they decided to go without one: they had to put in at Ryde to avoid French privateers: while they were there, Thomas was arrested for debt and the captain refused to carry Carey. He went to London and heard of a Danish ship, but its fare was too high: he dashed to North-ampton to raise more money, and finally, after countless difficulties, he and his wife (who had determined to come after all) set sail on 13 June 1797.

In those days missionaries could not land in India without a licence, and in that very year a member of parliament had declared that, so far from wishing to see 100,000 natives con-

[1] Thomas Thompson, a Fellow of Christ's College, Cambridge, suggested to the S.P.G. to work in Africa, and laboured himself in Guinea from 1751–7.

verted, he would lament such a circumstance as the most serious and fatal disaster that could happen.

Carey got the charge of an indigo factory near Calcutta, and was allowed to preach to his workpeople: he made no converts, but he learnt Bengali, and having bought a secondhand printing press, started to translate the Bible.

Four new missionaries came out, but there was trouble with the authorities, and they had to take refuge in a Danish settlement on the other side of the river: there Carey joined them, as he was not allowed to set up a printing press in the Company's territory. There, at Serampore, they produced a Bengali New Testament.

In 1801 Lord Wellesley, the Governor-General, founded a college to teach Indian languages, and made Carey professor of Bengali. Wellesley was a very great governor who had suppressed infanticide, and he sympathized with Carey's desire to see 'suttee' (the burning of widows with their dead husbands) abolished. But his term of office was ending, and his successor forbade all missionary preaching: 'the Governor-General does not interfere with the prejudices of the natives, and he must request Mr. Carey to abstain likewise from any interference with them'. But Lord Wellesley, now at home, took up their cause, and by 1813 parliament agreed to allow missionaries to enter India.

Meanwhile the printing went on: by 1808 they had mastered and used eight languages, and 20 years later the whole or part of the Bible had been translated into 44 languages and dialects: as Southey said, 'These low-born, low-bred mechanics have done more towards spreading the knowledge of the scriptures among the heathen than has been accomplished or even attempted by all the world besides.'

In 1829 came the greatest day of Carey's life: one Sunday morning a courier came to him, with an Order in Council to be translated into Bengali. Carey was a strict Sabbatarian, but a glance at the document showed him that on this occasion he must work on Sunday, for it was the Edict which abolished 'suttee' throughout the British Dominions in India.

His motto throughout life had been, 'Attempt great things for God; expect great things from God', and he is a noble figure to head the list of British missionaries of modern days.

The Dissenters were slightly ahead of Church people in their interest in missions, and the London Missionary Society was formed in 1795:[1] some of the Evangelical clergy joined, but felt that there was need for a society in direct connexion with their own Church. One of the men who was most influential in forming the Church Missionary Society in 1799 was CHARLES SIMEON of Cambridge (1759–1836). He, like others, ascribed his conversion to a text which he found when he opened the Bible in search of guidance: the text he found was 'Him they compelled to bear the cross'—and the fact that the words were written of Simon of Cyrene seemed to him a call: 'Henceforth', he said, 'I bind persecution as a wreath of glory round my head.'

He was persecuted at Cambridge, where his church-wardens who disapproved of him, locked the pew doors, and removed the benches which he brought in for the crowds which came to hear him, but he had a great influence there, and what was even more important, he induced William Wilberforce to take an interest in foreign missions. The Society was founded by sixteen clergymen and nine laymen, to be 'conducted on the church principle, but not on the High Church principle'—differing thus from the L.M.S. on one hand and the S.P.G. on the other.

The Archbishop of Canterbury was not enthusiastic: he would only promise 'to watch its proceedings with candour'. Its early proceedings were not impressive. After it had been in existence four years, though it was well supplied with money, it had to confess that it could find no man or woman ready to go as a missionary, and next year it had to be content with two German Lutherans who went to West Africa: after ten years they had sent out five, all Germans, one of whom had died and one been dismissed.

It should be remembered that their first efforts were made in West Africa, in the desire 'to make the best reparation in our power for the manifold wrongs inflicted' by the slave-trade, and that these missionaries had to work there, in days

[1] Another society which came into existence at this time was the British and Foreign Bible Society (1804).

before quinine or mosquito-nets, in a climate where it was very difficult for a European to survive.

As so much has been said of our great debt to the Methodist and Evangelical movements, it is right also to call attention to their defects.

Though the religious feelings which they aroused were unquestionably deep, they ran in a very narrow channel. They concentrated on emotion, and tended to despise reason, with the result that they produced no writings of lasting value: they hardly faced intellectual difficulties, opposed Biblical criticism, and despised what they called 'human science'. Their narrowness was also shown in their abhorrence of almost all forms of amusement and in their extreme Sabbatarianism. Sunday in their hands became a day of gloom, and the emphasis they laid on the thought of death was exaggerated.[1]

They bitterly opposed any relaxation of the laws against Roman Catholics; Wesley protested against it, and after the Protestant riots of 1780 (the Lord George Gordon riots) till 1829, most of the Evangelicals fought vigorously against any concession to them.

These were serious defects, which hampered religious progress and seemed to suggest that good Christian people were opposed to the cause of truth and justice, and only concerned with the saving of individual souls. They were not interested in the Church as a society, and made little use of its methods. It is very possible to care too much for religious institutions,

---

[1] Three quotations from great writers will show the tyranny of a false idea of Sunday, extending over a century. Dr. Johnson says: 'Sunday was a heavy day to me when I was a boy. My mother confined me on that day, and made me read *The Whole Duty of Man*, from a great part of which I could derive no instruction.' Ruskin writes in *Praeterita*: 'The horror of Sunday used even to cast its prescient gloom as far back in the week as Friday', while Dickens, in *Little Dorrit*, written in 1855, makes one of his characters speak of 'the dreary Sunday of his childhood, when he sat with his hands before him, scared out of his senses by a horrible tract . . . the sleepy Sunday of his boyhood, . . . the interminable Sunday of his nonage', leading up to 'the resentful Sunday of a little later, when he sat glowering and glooming through the tardy length of the day, with a sullen sense of injury in his heart'.

but it is equally possible to care for them too little; and the Evangelicals certainly made this mistake. Until the Oxford Movement began in 1833, this side of religion was dangerously neglected and a rather narrow type of personal piety prevailed in the Church.

This is perhaps the place to consider the difference between the High and Low Church parties as they were at the beginning of the century. The Low Church party, which was very much in the ascendant, cared little for history or for tradition; so that the government of the Church, and its seasons, meant little to them. The most marked difference at this time was in their attitude towards Episcopacy. The High Church party felt bishops to be an essential part of Church government, and, whether or not they could trace their descent from the Apostles, they were on sure ground in saying that they had behind them a tradition of seventeen hundred years. In their view they alone could ordain, and they alone could administer Confirmation, the service which admits those who receive it to Holy Communion.[1] This is why, in the mission field, they were anxious, as soon as possible, to see a 'diocese' established with a bishop in control, and why they tried so hard (and long without success) to get bishops appointed to look after Church people in America.

On this point the Evangelicals, or Low Churchmen, were rather inconsistent: though they were 'Churchmen', and therefore accepted government by bishops, they were little interested in having them appointed in foreign lands, and rather suspicious of them. The Dissenters, who did not approve of bishops at all, were on this point much more consistent.

It is pleasant to be able to add that (as we shall see later), the two great Church Missionary societies, the S.P.G. and the C.M.S., now work in perfect harmony and agreement, and it may also be said that in Christian foreign missions, where the need for unity is most obvious, real steps are now being taken, with general good will, to work out a scheme by which the greatest possible unity can be secured.

[1] Though different views are held as to the precise effect of infant baptism, all Christian bodies feel the need of a solemn service by which the young member accepts his responsibilities and is admitted to full membership.

XVII

A DEARTH OF GREAT MEN—TO 1833

In the first third of the nineteenth century there was not much organized activity among religious people. The reasons for this (apart from the normal weakness of human nature) are not difficult to see. The first 15 years were years of war, and when the war was over the social problems were not less pressing. It might truly be said that this was just the opportunity for Christian influence to make itself felt, but the opportunity was not taken. The French Revolution had been so strongly atheistic that most 'good', but not imaginative, people had come to regard all reformers as atheists, as some undoubtedly were, and they were more anxious to defend religion as an institution than to remove grievances. They all, Churchmen and Dissenters alike, were far too ready to accept the absurd argument: Radicals are infidels: Radicals want reform: therefore reform is an infidel notion.

A Christian is quite entitled to say that the reforms in the criminal code made at this time (from 1820) which, among other things, abolished the death penalty for a hundred crimes, were inspired by Christian principles: but he exposes himself to the retort that neither Bentham nor Romilly, who had most to do with them, was by any means orthodox Christians: the orthodox (of both kinds) were more concerned in resisting Catholic Emancipation, which was finally passed in 1829.

Here are, for example, some of the abuses which roused Romilly to take action. A pickpocket was condemned to death if he stole anything worth five shillings: so was any one who stole from a shop: in 1816 a boy of ten was in Newgate under sentence of death for this offence: a boy of fourteen had recently been hung for a crime of which he was in fact innocent. To be condemned to the hulks was feared almost as much as death, for there first offenders were herded with the worst criminals: there was a boy of eleven there in 1815, and eight under fifteen. Transportation was even worse, and was so stupidly inflicted that, though the voyage to Botany Bay took nine months, fifty convicts had recently been transported who had a year or less to serve.

The treatment of children under the Poor Law was atrocious. Poor children in London were shipped off in wagon loads to Lancashire cotton mills, and as a premium was paid for apprentices they were frequently murdered.

Such scandals as these, in which respectable people acquiesced, must make all Christian people wonder whether there are any similar scandals in which they acquiesce to-day.

The Church itself was badly in need of reform, and this was supplied, not, it must be confessed, at its own wish, by laws passed in 1836-8. The very large incomes of bishops, the number of cases where several livings were held by one man, and the scandal of non-residence, were all dealt with by parliament, to the great advantage of the Church and of religion in general.

Its leaders, though often good and generous men, were of the 'high and dry' type, and for the most part extremely conservative: the Evangelicals were still mainly interested in the negro problem (which occasioned Dickens' sarcastic picture of Mrs. Jellyby) and with the exception of Buxton had now no distinguished leaders.

It was a Quaker, ELIZABETH FRY, who in this period attempted the most purely Christian work which was done from a religious motive. She went one day to visit the female prisoners in Newgate: she found three hundred women, some convicted, some not yet tried, misdemeanants and felons, confined in two wards and two cells, sleeping on the bare floor, cooking, washing, eating, and sleeping in the same room. She formed a committee of ladies who visited the place: got the prisoners clothes and work to do: got a matron appointed: induced them to appoint monitors of their own to see that some simple rules of decency were kept, and in fact completely reformed the institution.

She spoke to them continually of religion, perhaps in language which would not attract us to-day, but it requires a good deal of courage to invite three hundred prisoners in such conditions to listen to preaching at all. The American ambassador said that Mrs. Fry in Newgate was a more wonderful sight than Westminster Abbey: and as in ten years time forty per cent. less of the female prisoners got into trouble again, her exhortations clearly had effect.

She did not limit her attention to Newgate: she found that female criminals condemned to transportation were first sent across England chained together with iron hoops round waist and legs and ankles; were then entirely neglected during the voyage to Botany Bay; and that there were no arrangements for looking after them when they got to New South Wales. She succeeded in completely changing this state of affairs.

She visited prisons in England and Scotland: in the latter country she found debtors kept half a dozen in a room nine foot square with one bed among the lot of them, and prisoners who had once tried to escape chained to an iron bar so ingeniously that they could never undress and never go to bed.

During the bad winter of 1819 she was so much impressed by the number of homeless wanderers in the London streets that she instituted the first night-shelter for the homeless.

These examples show that there was much obviously Christian work to be done, and increase our regret that the official representatives of Christianity seem to have been so blind to it.

On the other hand Christians deserve more credit than they usually get for being the first to urge (and to pay for) the education of the children of the country: we have seen the small beginnings of this in the eighteenth century, and in the early years of the nineteenth much more attention was paid to it. In 1808 the Lancasterian Association[1] (called after Lancaster, a Quaker) was founded, and the National Society (for Promoting the Education of the Poor in the Principles of the Established Church) in 1811.

Both societies accomplished a great deal for education, but very unfortunately they disagreed as to the kind of religious education which should be given, and the dispute between the supporters of different schemes prevented the government from taking the matter in hand till 1870.

As we look back, we can see that both sides were to blame and that though the disagreements were natural they ought to

[1] Afterwards (1814) called the British and Foreign School Society.

have been overcome: at the same time it is easy to understand and to sympathize with both points of view.

The Church people had spent a great deal of money in providing schools before the government took any interest in education: they naturally wanted to go on giving the kind of religious teaching in which they believed. The Noncon-formists, on the other hand, were afraid that their children would be 'converted' into 'churchmen' against their parents' wishes, and though many attempts were made, no scheme was found which would satisfy both sides.

Every one who believes that religion is the foundation of the national life must agree that it should be taught as well as possible (which must at least mean by people who believe in it, and can give reasons for their belief) and that a parent should, so far as possible, be able to get for his child the kind of religious education which he desires. With the better understanding which now exists, there is good reason to hope that this can be secured, and nothing would be gained by tracing the struggle which raged so long and with so much un-Christian bitterness.

Its result has been to rob Christians of some of the credit which, as has been said, they deserve for their service to national education, and, what is much more serious, to waste nearly a century in the teaching of religion. This was all the more unfortunate because it was at about this period that the nation began, without fully realizing it, to depart from the Christian traditions which had created and shaped it. Those traditions 'had been rooted in the Christian morality of the medieval Church which, believing that the purpose of life was to save and prepare man's soul for heaven, taught that worldly laws and institutions should be based as far as possible on the gospel of Christ' and, however much it failed in its practice, those traditions did 'make it easier for the ordinary citizen to live a Christian life and taught him to revere just and honest dealing'.[1]

The Reformation did not destroy those traditions, and it is significant that the king in his coronation oath still swears to 'do justice, stop the growth of iniquity, protect the Holy

[1] Bryant, *English Saga*, p. 31.

Church of God, help and defend widows and orphans, restore things that are gone to decay, maintain the things that are restored, punish and reform what is amiss, and confirm what is in good order.' The national character was known to be the national concern.

But new traditions had been growing up in the eighteenth century, and people were coming to think that human reason was so powerful by itself that belief in God was unnecessary. It was more and more believed that man by his own exertions could make himself and the world perfect, and (what was equally serious) that if every man was left free to follow his own interest the result would be 'the greatest happiness of the greatest number'.

It is easy to see how this new idea altered the situation. Christians wish to promote happiness, but they do not regard it as the chief object of existence: they may say 'if you are good you will be happy', but they do not say 'if you are happy you will be good'—and they add that if you aim *only* at happiness you are unlikely to get it.

Again, they are anxious to see people free, but they have always held that man is the servant of God, and that 'His service is perfect freedom': true freedom does not mean merely doing what you like.

What made things worse was that it came to be assumed that to make money is the shortest and safest road to happiness, and this is entirely an un-Christian idea, for the Christian view is that 'the love of money is a root of all kinds of evil'.

The wars with Napoleon prevented these eighteenth-century ideas from bearing fruit at first, but when war-time was over they mastered the country, and neither the Church nor the Nonconformists were strong enough to resist them. The nineteenth century became a time when it was thought to be the duty of man to get rich quick, and that by doing so he was doing his part as a good citizen.

England, as a whole, did get rich very quickly, but it was done at the expense of great suffering to the weak. The (un-Christian) idea that a man's only duty is to himself, combined with the (foolish) idea that government is only concerned with keeping people free, resulted in a policy called *laissez faire*, or 'leave things alone'. It was silly to say that a starving man was free to bargain about his wages or those of his wife and children: he had to take what he could get and the employer paid as little as the workman would take.

It is important to understand that this was approved by philosophers, and economists; and highminded men—John Bright, for instance—thought that to limit child labour was to interfere with the sacred law of supply and demand. It is not our business here to discuss how these ideas have gradually disappeared: our point is first, that our present troubles mainly come from abandoning the old Christian idea that government was concerned with the national character; and secondly, that everything which has been done by government to make people healthier, to educate them, and to give them a fair chance of securing a freedom which is worth having, has been a return to the old Christian tradition which the nineteenth century forgot.

XVIII

THE THREE EVENTS OF 1833

FROM a religious point of view the year 1833 is remarkable for three events, the triumphant end of the struggle against slavery, the passing of the first Factory Act, and the beginning of the Oxford Movement.

(1) BUXTON had been urging emancipation ever since 1823, when he asked the House of Commons to agree 'that slavery was repugnant to the principles of the British Constitution and of the Christian religion, and that it ought to be gradually abolished throughout the British Colonies': Canning then proposed as an amendment that the condition of slaves should immediately be improved, and this was carried. It had some effect, but the West Indies complained that they were being offered up as 'a propitiatory sacrifice at the altar of fanaticism' and that the present moment was 'peculiarly unfavourable' for doing anything of the kind.

For ten years little was done: the public flogging of female slaves still continued: the whip was still used in the field: a missionary suspected of sympathizing with the slaves was hounded to death, and when a man and his wife, convicted of the brutal murder of a young negress, were awarded five months' imprisonment, the planters of Jamaica protested against so harsh a sentence. The release of slaves who were the property of the Crown in 1831 led to a belief among the negroes that they were all to be free, and the rising which followed was suppressed with great cruelty.

At last, through Buxton's unceasing efforts, the government decided to take the matter in hand, and in 1833 Lord Stanley proposed that after an intermediate period of 12 years' apprenticeship all slaves should be free: the period was reduced to seven years, and the compensation which he proposed to give the planters was raised by five millions to £20,000,000. Slavery ceased on 1 August 1834: 'as the midnight hour struck in every place of worship in the West Indian colonies, the hymn of praise was raised to the God of the white man, the God of the black; the God of the free man, the God of the slave'.[1]

As another historian writes, 'The unweary, unostentatious, and inglorious crusade of England against slavery may probably be regarded as among the three or four perfectly virtuous pages comprised in the history of nations',[2] and it is to the Quakers and to the Evangelicals that the honour belongs.

(2) It was a great and ardent Evangelical, Lord Ashley, better known as LORD SHAFTESBURY, who had most to do with that working of the national conscience which produced the first Factory Act in 1833.[3] Children of eight or nine years old were then liable to work 13 hours a day (except in cotton factories where the hours were limited to 69 a week): the conditions were as bad as possible and nothing was done to safeguard health. The Act of 1833 limited child labour to eight hours a day.[4]

[1] Walpole, *History of England*, iii, 198.   [2] Lecky, *European Morals*, i, 153.
[3] Sadler, a Tory member, had first raised the question in 1831, and got a committee appointed to investigate it.
[4] The mines were as bad as the factories: in 1831 20,000 miners from Northumberland and Durham gathered to demand (among other things) that no boy should work more than 12 hours a day: children of six and eight were among those then employed.

In 1840 it was forbidden to employ children in sweeping chimneys (a reform associated with Charles Kingsley and the *Water Babies*) and in the same year Ashley secured the appointment of a commission to report on their employment in mines. It reported in 1842 and showed that while children were usually employed at seven, in many districts they started work much younger: they were brutally treated, given no care and no education. Ashley introduced a bill forbidding their employment under 13 years and this was passed, with the compromise that boys of ten might work three days a week.

He was asked, 'Where will you stop?' and his answer was, 'Nowhere, so long as any portion of this mighty evil remains to be removed.' He continued his efforts both to secure some education for children and to limit all labour to ten hours a day, and by 1847 had succeeded.[1]

Lord Shaftesbury has been described as 'one of the purest and noblest characters on the political stage' and as having 'led a long and consistent life of laborious self-denial, devoted to the spiritual and material welfare of his fellow-creatures.'[2] He was narrow in his religious views, denounced anything that was liberal in theology, and was a violent Sabbatarian. But his successful efforts on behalf of children and workers generally, the reforms which he secured in the management of asylums, and his ceaseless interest in all good causes, entitle him to a very high place among those whose love for man has been inspired by their love for God.

(3) The third event of 1833 was of a very different kind—it was the preaching by John Keble of a sermon on National Apostasy, which was the starting-point of the OXFORD MOVEMENT.

We have lately been dealing with practical reforms, and this may have left the impression that they are the only things with which Christianity is concerned. But though no Christian ought ever to forget his duty to his neighbour (as most of them

[1] It may be noted that the Whigs, including, very strangely, John Bright, strongly opposed these reforms, and that the Tories, including the bishops, strongly supported them.

[2] Paul, *History of Modern England*, i, 71.

did then and do still), he is also concerned with religious truth, and the Oxford Movement was quite right in calling attention to some sides of it which had been much neglected.

The Evangelicals, as we have said, were only interested in the individual soul: they had no care for history, and were not concerned with the life of the Christian society. They were violently and uncharitably anti-Roman, had opposed all concessions to Roman Catholics, and were inclined to regard any revival of old Church customs and traditions as disloyal to the Church of England.

On the other side, the Tractarians,[1] as they came to be called, had no difficulty in pointing out

(a) That Christ undoubtedly founded a society to which His followers were to belong, and that no society can flourish without agreed rules which all its members keep.

(b) That the Church of England had always maintained that it was truly a Catholic Church, and had broken with Rome precisely because Rome had introduced in the course of the Middle Ages ideas and practices which were *not* Catholic or ancient (cf. p. 105).

(c) That it was absurd to suppose that by reviving customs and practices of the ancient and undivided Church they intended any disloyalty to the Church of England. The Reformation had been made at a time of great excitement, and it was probable, or indeed certain, that some good things had then been needlessly swept away. The Church of England had not (as the Roman Catholics maintained) been the creation of Henry VIII, but was in fact the truest representative of the oldest Christian tradition.

In estimating the effects of a religious movement it is always safer to take the views of those who look at it from a detached point of view. We will therefore quote a few sentences from two very un-clerical historians. 'The Oxford Movement produced a most laudable increase of activity among parochial

---

[1] The name was derived from the *Tracts for the Times* which they published; the most famous (No. 90) argued that the Thirty-nine Articles did not prevent a loyal Churchman from holding views which they seemed to condemn. It should be remembered that the authors of those Articles had in some cases purposely used ambiguous language in order to win as much agreement as possible (see p. 86).

clergymen. The Bishops felt the pressure of a vigilant criticism, and did their best to raise the standard.'[1] 'It galvanized
the religious world into vitality, and the stimulus which it has
given to religion has been felt by bodies widely dissenting
from the Tractarians. High Churchmen and Low Churchmen, Nonconformists and Roman Catholics have all made an
effort, such as was never made before, to infuse religious
activity into the nation.'[2]

Its external effects have been obvious in the greater care
taken of churches, in the revival (not always wise) of Gothic
architecture, in the improvement of Church music, and in
greater attention to the forms of worship generally, and in the
recovery of the true meaning of Sunday which the Sabba-
tarians had obscured. In all these respects Nonconformists
have also benefited.

They have not been so much affected by its sacramental
teaching, and they are not ready to accept the extreme
emphasis which the Tractarians laid on the importance of the
Episcopate—often in such a way as to seem to suggest that
those who rejected it were hardly true Christians at all. It is
quite possible to hold that Apostolic succession is an historic
fact without drawing from it all the conclusions which the
Tractarians drew: the Church in the seventeenth century
would certainly not have agreed with them.[3]

JOHN KEBLE (1792–1866) was a brilliant scholar who was
content to retire from Oxford to a Hampshire parsonage, but
from Hursley he exercised a commanding influence on the
movement. He was satisfied that the Prayer Book contained
all the 'Catholic' doctrines which he valued, and that the
ancient traditions which he wished to see restored were all
the legitimate inheritance of the Church of England. His book
of Poems, the *Christian Year*, was very widely read and had

[1] Paul, op. cit., i, 17.   [2] Walpole, op. cit., iv, 439.
[3] The Archbishops' Committee on Doctrine in the Church of England
says: 'We do not doubt that God has accepted and used other ministries
which through breach of continuity are deficient in outward authorization;
but we are convinced that the Anglican communion has been right to regard
the historic Episcopate as in a special sense the organ of unity and continuity.' (p. 122.)

The Tractarians would have found it difficult to accept wholeheartedly
the first of these sentences.

enormous influence: his morning and evening hymns ('New every morning' and 'Sun of my soul') are known to all churchgoers, and those who use them or the Whitsuntide hymn 'When God of old came down from heaven' will appreciate the simple and serious faith of the writer. His character was among the greatest assets of the Tractarians.

JOHN HENRY NEWMAN (1801–90) was the genius of the movement, and his submission to Rome in 1845 was the greatest blow it could have received. It seemed to justify all the suspicions of those who had opposed it from the beginning. Newman took with him several of his friends and supporters, but the unwavering constancy of Keble and Pusey saved the situation. Newman was a great man and a great writer, facts which can be appreciated even by those who feel his search for external authority un-Christian and the logic of his arguments extremely narrow. Two of his hymns, 'Praise to the Holiest' and 'Lead, kindly light' are known and valued by all English Christians.

The Tractarians were bitterly attacked, not only by the Evangelicals who called them Romanizers (especially after Newman's secession), but also by what is called the Broad Church party. These were liberal-minded clergymen such as F. D. Maurice, Thomas Arnold, Charles Kingsley, and laymen like Tom Hughes and Ludlow (see p. 174). They were liberals in politics and did much for social reform, some of them being the first to be called Christian Socialists.[1] Maurice did much for working-men's colleges, Arnold was a leader in the reform of public schools and inspired many of his pupils with his liberal ideas. Kingsley in his novels *Alton Locke* and *Yeast*, showed real sympathy with the poor, and was himself a supporter of the Chartist Movement.

But they were also liberals in theology, and were not prepared to accept the rigid definitions of the Tractarians, believing that the unity of Christians rested on wider foundations: but their liberalism also greatly shocked Evangelicals like Lord Shaftesbury.

---

[1] Their leading principle was that the law of Christ ought to rule economic practice: they denounced sweating, and the Co-operative Movement owes much to them.

It must not be thought that these were merely internal disputes of the Church: they affected all Christians. For nearly a century there had been little real learning shown in the religious world, and it was very important that Christians should show that they regarded the discovery of truth as of real importance. As we have seen, the Methodists and the Evangelicals had concentrated mainly on the emotions (see p. 145): it was high time that Christians of all kinds should try to think out their position, and naturally the task was difficult.

One great difficulty concerned the Bible: was it to be regarded as verbally inspired? was it right to study it, like any other ancient book, in the light of the new knowledge brought by history and science? The Methodists and the Evangelicals were both very conservative, and so, in a different way, were the Tractarians. The Broad Church clergy may have made many mistakes and been loose in their statements, but they have the great honour of having shown that Christians ought to inquire fearlessly not only into the Bible, but into all things, and to welcome truth from whatever quarter it may come. It is ultimately due to them that Christians of every kind, Nonconformists as well as Churchmen, have co-operated in the study both of the Bible and of Christian doctrine.

This is not the place in which to discuss the disputes and conclusions of critics and scholars: they naturally do not always agree in their conclusions, but there has in the last century been a far freer inquiry into all such matters, a very general agreement as to method, a real co-operation between scholars of different types, and a certainty that to find truth is one of the first of Christian duties.[1]

[1] For example, there are few Christians nowadays who doubt (1) that the book of Genesis does not give, and was never meant to give, a scientific account of the origin of the world; (2) that the chief value of the Old Testament lies in the way in which the Jews were guided to a true view of God; (3) that some of their earlier views of God were false and were gradually discarded, so that we need feel no surprise that we find actions attributed to Him which are quite inconsistent with His character as revealed by Christ; (4) that all parts of the Bible are not on the same spiritual level; (5) that a prophet's main glory lies not in his *foresight* into the future but in his *insight* into God's purposes. But all this agreement, and much of a similar kind, has only been reached after fierce disputes in which the pioneers came in for much abuse.

XIX

A CENTURY OF CHRISTIAN WORK ABROAD
1833–1933

THERE are obvious difficulties in giving anything like a history of Christianity in the last century, for we are dealing not with events which can be chronicled but with what is going on in the mind and heart of the nation, and this can hardly be set out in chronological order. It seems better therefore to take the three sides of Christian life suggested by the three events of 1833, and to deal in turn with Christian work abroad, with Christian work at home (limiting that for the moment to what is called 'philanthropy'), and lastly with the development of Christian thought and practice.

There is nothing more encouraging in the history of English religion than the amazing growth of the interest in foreign missions in the last century. If any one objects that this can hardly be described as Christianity *in* England, the answer is simple: there can be few better proofs that a man values his religion than that he is really anxious to hand it on to those who have not known it. This is what we should expect if it is really 'good news', which is what the word 'gospel' means.

There are two rough tests which we can apply—the amount of money which Christian people are willing to give for the purpose, and the number who are willing to serve themselves: judged by either test, the change in a hundred years is wonderful. Here are some figures, as accurate as we can make them. (The figures given in both cases deal only with societies existing in 1833, and take no account of bodies such as the Universities Mission to Central Africa, or the China Inland Mission, which have come into existence since.)

(1) *Money*. In 1833 the total amount given by this country to (non-Roman) missions was about £120,000:

in 1933 the amount given to the same societies was about
£1,420,000.[1]

(2) *Men.* As we have seen, in its early days the Church
Missionary Society could find no man or woman in the British
Isles ready to go abroad in its service. By 1833, there were
hardly more than 200 missionaries working for all the (non-
Roman) societies then existing: by 1933 the number had risen
to at least 3,000—and this takes no account of many thousands
of lay native workers, nor of the wives of missionaries, who
are often missionaries in all but name.[2]

It will be asked what are the results of all this activity?
Before we try to answer this question, we must bear two things
in mind. The first is that no good missionary wants to reckon
up converts like so many scalps: he knows, much better than
we do, how often conversion may be only nominal: and the
second, that much Christian work, as for instance in hospitals,
is not directly aimed at 'conversion' but at spreading a knowledge of the virtues for which Christianity stands, and improving the conditions under which the heathen live. These
are things which cannot appear in statistics, but it is worth
while to remember what was said by Robert Louis Stevenson
—by no means an orthodox Christian—'Those who deblater-
ate against missions have only one thing to do, to come and
see them on the spot.'

But for the benefit of those who cannot do this we must give
a few figures, remembering that some 70 years ago a leader-
writer in *The Times* said, 'An ordinary Englishman has seen
almost every human or brute native of foreign climes, but few
can say that they have seen a missionary or a Christian
convert.'

Here then are some figures. The number of communicants
in Africa and Asia (excluding the Roman Communion) was
nearly four million and a half in 1938, which incidentally is

[1] It should, in fairness, be remembered how greatly the national income
has increased since 1833: for that reason the facts concerning the number
of missionaries are the more important.

[2] All these statistics necessarily omit the work done by Roman Catholics:
their zeal for missions has always been great, and until the last century it put
the Reformed Churches—or certainly the English Reformed Churches—
to shame.

more than four times as many as in 1903. The number of baptized in the Anglican Communion alone amounts to nearly two million and a quarter, and those of other Christian Communions (again excluding the Roman Catholics) to seven million and a half.[1]

One more set of figures shows that Christianity is no longer a European export, but has really found a home of its own in heathen lands, for native Christians in the dioceses helped by the Church of England now raise themselves over £1,000,000 a year—nearly as much as they receive from us—and they provide more than 2,000 ordained ministers of their own and 20,000 native teachers.[2]

It would be silly to exaggerate the importance of these figures, but it is perfectly plain that they do represent an amazing Christian achievement in the course of a century. Let us turn from dry statistics to look at a few examples of Christian missions in action.

We will begin with AFRICA, as that was the country to which our first missionary energy was directed. The first missionaries sent out by the C.M.S. were not 'successful': Sierra Leone was known as 'the White Man's Grave', and twelve out of fourteen were dead in 18 months: but they laid a fine foundation.

A great name in African history is that of *David Livingstone* (1813–73). As his epitaph in Westminster Abbey says, 'For 30 years his life was spent in an unwearied effort to evangelize the Native Races, to explore the Undiscovered Secrets, to abolish the Desolating Slave Trade of Central Africa, where with his last words he wrote, "All I can add in my solitude is: May Heaven's rich blessing come down on every one, American, English, or Turk, who will help to heal this open sore of the world." '

There is no space to tell the story of his crusade against the slave-trade (which, as he estimated, killed from four-fifths to nine-tenths of those who were captured, before they even

[1] These latter figures include those for aborigines in Australia, New Zealand, and Oceania.

[2] These last are 'Anglican' figures: other 'Protestant' Communions provide more than 12,000 in the native ministry and nearly 80,000 native teachers.

reached slavery) nor how he roused the hatred of Arabs, Boers, and Portuguese. He travelled up rivers blocked with dead bodies which the crocodiles would not eat, for they had already had so much of that food: he had seen negro children, trotting by the side of the slave gangs, droop and die of a broken heart when they heard the songs and dances in a free village which they passed.

He died, with no white companion near him, in Central Africa, and there are few stories more heroic than that which tells how six of his native followers carried his body 1,200 miles through swamps, deserts, and hostile tribes, so that it could rest in Westminster Abbey at last.

On his last visit to England he said, 'I go back to Africa to make an open path for commerce and for Christianity: do you carry out the work which I have begun: I leave it with you.'

So far as Christianity is concerned, his words had their effect. Five years after his death, Stanley, the traveller who had been to look for him, wrote a letter to the *Daily Telegraph* telling of new tribes which he had discovered and appealing for some missionary to go. In five months eight men had started, a sailor, two engineers, a curate, an architect, a doctor, an artisan, and a builder. (You will observe that Christian missions are not solely concerned with preaching.) A little more than a year later two men, one nearly blinded by an arrow, the other wounded in the arm, set foot in Uganda; one of the party had been left in charge of the baggage, the rest were dead or invalided home. By the end of the year two of the surviving three had been martyred.

But the seed had been sown, and the blood of martyrs is what makes it grow. It was seven years before the first bishop (Hannington) was consecrated: he was captured and speared to death before he reached Uganda. Within a few weeks of the arrival of the news in England 50 recruits had offered for foreign service. Meanwhile in Uganda the king had gone on his way: three Christian native boys were slowly burnt to death. It is a glorious and dramatic fact that 25 years later a granite cross was set up in their memory in the presence of a company representing seventy thousand native Christians.

It is an equally dramatic fact, and one even more closely

connected with Livingstone, that to-day a Christian cathedral built by freed slaves stands on the site of the old slave-market in Zanzibar.

If we look at INDIA, we ought to do so remembering that in 1805 a great governor-general said that you might as well fire a pistol into a powder magazine as allow a missionary to preach in India. There are now some three million native Christians in India who owe their conversion to the Reformed Churches, with three native bishops working side by side with those of British birth, and on perfect equality with them. The Simon Report (which is not a missionary document) gives them high praise. It says, for instance, that more than one in five of them can read and write, a figure far higher than the average, although a great many of them come from the 'depressed classes': it says that the Christians are the only people who have really tried to tackle the problem of the Untouchables who make up nearly a third of the Hindu population, and finally that they have done all this without offending the susceptibility of Moslem or Hindu, and live at peace with their neighbours. This is an achievement of which any English Christian may be proud. Let us follow this up with two examples of how Christianity works: first let us look at a school in Kashmir.

The Kashmiri is not highly thought of by most Europeans, who consider him deficient in manliness. When this C.M.S. school was started no boy would willingly play football, swim, or handle an oar: shorts were called 'Christianity clothing': all exercise was thought degrading and any form of social service unthinkable. The change is perfectly astounding: the boys now climb mountains (thought to be the haunt of demons), they swim lakes (thought to be infested by evil spirits): their regattas are one of the sights of the town. But what is still more remarkable is that they use their new-found powers to help other people: twelve boys, for instance, received life-saving medals in a recent year (and two were disqualified because they reported the matter themselves). They take out sick people on the river, they run the only fire brigade in the city, they volunteered to clean some of it when it was visited by cholera; some Hindu boys actually faced pollution and loss of caste by removing the body of a dead dog which had lain in the street for three days. They help overburdened coolies, they care for neglected children and neglected animals, and the school has even faced the scandal of child widows who are forbidden to marry again.

All this eminently Christian work has been carried out in a city where there was no tradition whatever of social service, and the bitterest religious and social divisions. No figures are published of 'conversions' but it is difficult to overestimate what the religious effect has been.[1]

No figures, and indeed no words, can do justice to the medical work done by men and women doctors for the men and women of India. It is all Christian in its inspiration and most of it is financed by Christian people in this country. One story will show something at least of the spirit which lies behind it: some hundred years or more ago a young English officer was taken prisoner by the Afghans: he was offered his life if he would deny his faith, but when he refused was brutally treated and murdered. It happened that he kept in a Testament a short diary of his last days, and many years later, after strange adventures, this book came into his sister's hands. She founded a bed in a frontier hospital for the use of the Afghans who are wounded in their frequent border feuds. The inscription over the bed is 'The Christian's revenge', and it may well be that it has caused some patients to inquire what Christianity is. The same question cannot but come to the minds of those whom these Christian doctors and nurses help, and their work may often be as eloquent as any sermon.

In CHINA, the Church of England was comparatively late in the field, but the L.M.S. (Congregationalists) went there in 1807, and it was a great L.M.S. missionary (Morison) who first translated the Bible into Chinese. The American Congregationalists came in 1830, and the Methodist Episcopal Church of America is very strong. The C.M.S. arrived in 1844 and the S.P.G. in 1874: there are now seven Chinese

[1] Two or three local rules are amusing: a boy who talks too much is put on the 'parrot bench' and made to go on talking ; a vain boy has to spend his time looking into a mirror; while a boy who uses foul language at a football match may have to stand for some time 'in a prominent place with his tongue out to allow the fresh air to clean it'.

bishops and 282 priests whereas 70 years ago there were two European bishops and one Chinese priest.

Christians in China have had more than their share of persecution: tens of thousands were put to death during the Boxer rising, but during the eight years which followed it more Chinese became Christians than during the 80 years before it.

In the midst of a war which has lasted more than four years a Chinese Christian can say of that young Church 'Christianity is seen at its best in times of danger and crisis', and General Chiang Kai-Shek, himself a fearless Christian, has coined the fine phrase 'Suffering is achievement'.

In their plans for a new order after the war the Chinese are receiving help and advice from the missionaries. A leading Chinese journal emphatically says that the war has shown, 'that whatever doubts may have existed in the past, the Christian missions in China fully and indisputably justify their existence. . . . They have definitely found their place in the life of the nation, fulfilling great human needs in its time of deepest travail.' Last year the Church in China gave more to missionary work than ever before.

The Church in China no longer feels that Christianity, with its message of triumph in suffering, is a foreign creed. She has taken it as her own. Slowly she is making rituals and forms of worship in which she feels at home: slowly she is creating her own hymns and melodies and her own theology, painfully finding her own words and terms as the truth burns into her soul.[1]

The story of a Christian Chinese school founded by the daughter of an ancient Chinese family gives some idea of the difficulties of the present day. *Miss Tseng*, who had been taught by the C.M.S., came to England to finish her education and went back in 1917. She found the Chinese Empire turned into a modern republic, and her own province the centre of civil war, but quite undaunted she started her school, taking as its motto 'Loyalty and sympathy', and giving it the name of the Garden of Fragrance.

Nine years later the Communists drove her away for six months, but the school went on, refusing to join in strikes or

[1] Galbraith, *New Life in China*.

anti-foreign demonstrations. Next year, when anti-Christian riots became more serious still, it carried on for three months after every other Christian school in Central China had been forced to close.

At last the Communists prevailed: the girls were given two hours in which to pack and go: they held their last school meeting and sang 'Onward, Christian soldiers', before marching out; at the gate they stopped to call out, 'The spirit of this school shall never die'.

And their prophecy came true: when peace came, they started again with little furniture and few books, as their property had all been burnt; in 1930 the Red Army came again and destroyed all they had left. But the school was not beaten: three of its students sailed to England to qualify as teachers and came back, refusing better paid work, to help Miss Tseng to plant the Garden of Fragrance for a third time. Five years ago there were 150 girls in it—and whatever may have happened since, English Christians may feel proud of having inspired so gallant an enterprise.

It is difficult at the moment to speak about JAPAN, for the Japanese are now as 'nationalistic' as the Germans, and do not like a religion which preaches the brotherhood of all mankind. Before the war, there was a self-governing church there with three Japanese bishops and more than 200 Japanese clergy. They must find it as hard as German Christians have found it to reconcile loyalty to their country with loyalty to their creed. But even if they decide to cut themselves off from other Christians (as seems sadly probable) the influence of Christianity has already been great: it has inspired a great deal of social reform, especially under a very remarkable man called *Kagawa*[1]

Kagawa (born in 1888) belongs to a wealthy Japanese family, which drove him out when, as a boy, he became a Christian. At the age of 21 he determined to go and live in the slums of Kobe, where 10,000 people then lived in the most appalling conditions. For 15 years he lived in a hut six feet square,

[1] Any one who is interested in the Japanese reaction to Christianity should read a fascinating book, *A Gentleman in Prison* (S.C.M.). The hero, a convicted murderer, was converted and his life entirely changed by reading Christ's words from the Cross.

ceaselessly preaching the love of God to beggars, thieves, murderers, and criminals of every description. And, like St. Francis, he lived up to his preaching, giving away everything, even the clothes he wore, to those in need, visiting the sick, comforting the sorrowful, feeding the hungry, and lodging the homeless. He suffered much violence and his life was often in danger.

In time he became Japan's first labour leader, and though he always urged constitutional ways of reform he was often in prison as an agitator and a pacifist: but all the reforms which have helped the townspeople and the peasants are due to him. He became a well-known writer, giving away almost all that he earned, even after his marriage: his wife on their wedding day (he is now an ordained minister) was brought home to a hut which already housed nine destitute persons of all ages.

Here are a few of his sayings and writings:

God is love! I will proclaim this till I fall, God is love! I do not mean that the unseen God is love. Where love is, there is God.

Christianity started the fight for personal purity in Japan ... Christianity taught our people social welfare work and public service.

Money corrupts men. I do not ask for money. Send us your love. Send us men who incarnate that love. Provide buildings that will symbolize love. If none of these things is possible, offer up passionate prayer on our behalf.

The future will find the Christians of Japan valiant and victorious defenders of the Cross.

When we turn to New Zealand we see another kind of Christian work—the protection of native races from oppression. *Samuel Marsden* was the second of the chaplains sent out to Botany Bay, where he had to contend with 'the vilest imaginable iniquities, the grossest abuses of authority and the most shameless licentiousness shielded by official influence.' But besides his work in Australia he visited New Zealand, and in 1808 came to England to plead for the Maori.

Many people in New Zealand thought the only thing to do with the Maoris was to exterminate them, but the missionaries thought otherwise, and it is due to them that Maoris hold their present place in New Zealand life. It was an uphill struggle, for they had to deal with civil wars among the people and with occasional outbreaks against the white man, but the influence of Marsden, of *Henry Williams* (an ex-officer in the Navy who had been ordained) and after 1841 of a great bishop, *G. A. Selwyn*, not only saved the Maoris, but carried out their purpose 'to bring the noble but benighted race of New Zealanders into the enjoyment of the light and freedom of the Gospel'.

This led to a more romantic enterprise. Bishop Selwyn was convinced that every Christian diocese ought to be a missionary one, and as (by an accident of drafting) his diocese included the Melanesian Islands, he persuaded New Zealand to undertake their conversion. This led to the foundation of a new diocese of Melanesia in 1861, and *Patteson* became its first bishop. Its work was carried on necessarily in small boats, and was full of dangers both from shipwrecks and from the hostility of natives armed with poisoned arrows. The hostility was mainly due to the kidnapping of natives for labour which was practically slavery, and led to the bishop's death in 1871. He landed alone on an island where he was murdered in revenge for five men recently kidnapped: two of the men in the boat which was waiting for him were wounded and died of lockjaw.

The story has a beautiful end. One of the wounded men decided to go and look for the bishop: as they rowed in, two canoes came towards them, one rowed by two women. As they drew near they cast off the other canoe which bore his body reverently laid out with five wounds on it, and a palm branch with five knots.

The palm branch is now a treasured possession of the S.P.G. House in London, and on the island there stands a cross with an inscription in memory of 'John Coleridge Patteson, whose life was here taken by men for whose sake he would willingly have given it.' It should be added that there are now 61 Melanesian clergy, more than three times as many as at the beginning of the century.[1]

---

[1] There has been no space to tell of the work done in the South Seas by the Wesleyans, the Congregationalists, and the Presbyterians, who number altogether far more members than the Anglicans, but they must certainly be remembered by any one who cares for heroism and unselfishness shown in the greatest of causes.

As representative of the great work done by medical missionaries let us take *Wilfred Grenfell* (1865-1940)—Grenfell of Labrador, knighted for his great services to that country. After working for some time with the North Sea fishermen, he sailed for Labrador in 1892 and devoted the rest of his life to the fishermen and natives of that land. The story of his adventures by sea and land, and of his struggles to improve conditions there, is a thrilling one and should be read in his own words. We can only summarize it by a brief quotation, 'love builds for a future, however remote; and at present we see no other way than to work for it, and know of no better means than to insure the permanency of the hospitals, orphanages, schools, and the industrial and co-operative enterprises, than to hasten, however little, the coming of Christ in Labrador.'

All these things owe their existence to Grenfell, and he says that, as his work drew towards an end, he 'believed more than ever that to follow Jesus Christ is the only real adventure of life.' In his case the inspiration is as clear as the results to which it has led.

These few illustrations give some idea of the variety of Christian work done by English people abroad in the last century, but they give no idea of its amount. It would be easy to multiply them. We have said nothing, for instance, of the work done for lepers in Nigeria, or for the blind in Burma, or of the Caravan Mission in the back parts of Canada: we have said nothing of the change to be seen in whole villages in India when they come over in a body to the Christian faith; nor of the invaluable work done by missionaries in translating the Bible and getting unknown languages into some grammatical shape,[1] and the few names of martyrs which we have given are a tiny fraction of those who have given their lives for the cause.[2]

But at least enough has been said to show that, so far as work abroad is concerned, English Christianity has been far more active and more enthusiastic than at any other period

[1] The work of the S.P.G. for instance, is done in 54 different languages.
[2] Those who wish for more such stories may be recommended to read *Pioneers of the Kingdom* (Highway Press).

of its history, and that is something which may comfort us when we see failures nearer home.

There are two or three other things which may encourage us. In the first place, the attitude of Christians to the heathen world has changed enormously for the better. We are no longer inclined to class them all together as equally ignorant of God, but are anxious to see in what ways their old faiths come near to any part of the truth and to welcome any such approach. It is silly to laugh at the comparatively small numbers who are converted from any highly developed faith: it cannot be easier for a Hindu or a Mohammedan to join us than it would be for us to join them. And it is equally silly to sneer at the numbers of comparatively ignorant people who become Christians: after all, that was a sneer levelled at St. Paul's converts. Missionaries are fighting on two fronts— trying to convince learned critics with an ancient faith of their own; and trying to raise to a decent life those whose religion has done them little but harm. They do not confuse the tasks, and neither should we.

Again it is a great encouragement to feel that Christian missionaries are increasingly ready to work together and to forget, so far as they honestly can, the things which divide them.[1] It is quite natural, considering the history of religion in England, that some English Christians, even within the Church, should put the emphasis in different places. The S.P.G. and the C.M.S. for example began, and for some time worked, on very different lines. But to-day they publish a common statement of their work under the pleasant name of 'Partners'.

It is not so easy for those who disbelieve in the value of bishops, or of set forms of prayer, to work in harmony with those who value them, and there are obvious difficulties when a very different view is taken of the Sacraments: all that can be said is that real efforts are being made in the mission field to find a solution of those difficulties, and that the prospect is much brighter than it ever has been.

[1] From this we have sorrowfully to exclude the Roman Catholics who are so certain that they are right and all other Christians wrong that their conscience too often forbids them to work together.

All Christians can unite in giving thanks for the memory of such men as Father Damien who ministered to the lepers in Molokai, Dr. Schweitzer, the somewhat unorthodox scholar and brilliant musician, who gave up everything to serve the lowest tribes in West Africa, or General Gordon praying for the Moslems who surrounded him in Khartoum. The name of Carey, the Baptist cobbler, is honoured side by side with that of Selwyn, the Etonian bishop, and those who remember the martyrdom of Bishop Patteson do not forget the fifteen, most of them members of the Zenana mission, who died in the massacre of Kuchang in 1895.

Whether or not they would all call themselves members of the Catholic Church, all missionaries are life members of a truly 'Catholic' society.

XX

A CENTURY OF CHRISTIAN WORK AT HOME
1833–1933

IT is much more difficult to give an idea of the philanthropic work which has been done by Christians at home in the last hundred years, for though there has been a great deal of it, and though it has all been Christian in origin, comparatively little has been done by Christian organization.

Lord Shaftesbury's work has been followed up in numerous directions but seldom for such definitely Christian reasons. The early leaders of the Trade Union Movement were very frequently Methodist preachers, but their work was mainly political. The Christian Socialist Movement, founded by Maurice and Kingsley, has been carried on with increasing vigour by great men such as Westcott, Scott Holland, and Bishop Gore: under the name of the Industrial Christian Fellowship it continues to urge the duty of Christians to have a social programme. *Bishop Westcott* of Durham, the first president of the Christian Social Union, played a large part in the settlement of a great miners' strike in 1892. The great movement known as the *Salvation Army*, at the other end of the religious scale, has won the respect of all for its unselfish care for the poor, and the Church Army has paid it the compliment of imitation. Countless Christian men and women have given their lives to social service, and there is more genuine sympathy with distress shown by every kind of religious body than at any time in our history. Very many so-called Christians fail to show any such interest, but that has been true in every period of Christian history, and the encouraging fact is that the interest is so general.

If we ask why this has produced no definitely Christian programme the answer is twofold. The first is, no doubt, that the divisions of Christendom hamper it, and make it difficult to form or to carry out a common plan. The second is that there is good reason to doubt how far it is right for Christians, as such, to organize themselves into the sort of political party which can get reforms carried. Let us look at this second answer a little more closely, remembering that our history shows that no religious body has ever joined a political party without losing much of its religion in the process.[1]

Christ did not lay down a social or political programme: He never, for instance, said a word about slavery, though it cannot be doubted that it was His influence which finally caused slavery to disappear. In the same way, He never spoke of the position of women, but the fact that He treated them on an equality with men, and chose many of them for His friends, was no doubt the reason why in Christian countries (and only there) the equality of women with men has been conceded. In both cases it was His unspoken word which ultimately brought the change.

It may be that it is the first duty of the Christian preacher to stir the conscience of his hearers to try to see how Christ's principles should be applied rather than himself to lay down a programme of reform. This does not mean that he should not have and express strong views of his own, as many Christians have done, to the great benefit of the country, but

[1] At different times in the century both the Church and the Nonconformists have made this mistake.

it does explain why such men have not more often taken the lead in large schemes of general reform.

It is only in so far as this country is a Christian country and really believes in the Fatherhood of God and the brotherhood of man that it is likely to care much about social conditions: it is more important that the nation's faith should be preserved than that particular reforms should be carried out, for there is always a danger that people will think that the chief object of religion is to make them comfortable, certainly in this world, and possibly in the next.

The Christian is bound to agitate for such things as better housing, but he is bound also to remember that better housing will not itself bring the Kingdom of God, and that his first duty is to proclaim that Kingdom. We are all democrats nowadays, but we do not all remember that the only sensible reason for being a democrat is the belief that man is the child of God: one man differs greatly from another in ability and character: it is only because men are all children of God that it is safe to trust them with power.

There are two very important questions to be faced in the period of reconstruction after the war: how can we ensure that the working people of this country are properly housed and paid and fed? How can we ensure that they understand the nature of the Christian God and what His service involves? People may differ as to which question is the more urgent and important, but no one can deny that it is the Christians who are most concerned to find an answer to the second.

This digression may have done something to explain why it is hard to say precisely what is due to Christianity in the social reforms of the last century: there is a real sense in which it can claim them all, and Christians will not be unduly perturbed if they are reminded that now, as in other centuries, many of the most Christian reforms have been accomplished by men who would not claim the Christian name.

But let us give a few more instances of individual Christians who have done great things for social reform. *Florence Nightingale* (1820–1910) is famous for her work in the Crimea, but it is not always remembered that she was a great reformer of hospitals at home and the founder of modern nursing. She was the daughter of rich parents, and though she felt that 'God called her to His service' when she was only seventeen, it was not till she was thirty that she decided to 'put away childish things—vain things—thoughts of love and marriage'.

In a year she had made up her mind to seek training as a nurse, and by 1854 she was superintendent of an Establishment for Gentlewomen during illness, in Harley Street, and not finding it easy to work under a committee.

The Crimean War gave her the opportunity of working on more independent lines, and in 1854 she set out in charge of 38 nurses to Scutari. Every one has heard of 'the lady with the lamp', and how she was adored by the soldiers whom she served, but not every one knows of the violence of the struggle which she urged (supported by the Minister for War, Sidney Herbert) against incompetence, red tape, the jealousy of religious sects, and human folly in every shape.[1] Her methods may have been drastic, but it was not long before she had reduced the death rate of the army from 42 per cent. to 2 per cent. of the cases treated in hospital.

After the Crimea she did not forget the soldier, and did much for the health of the Indian Army, but her main work was in the reform of hospitals at home, and in the training of nurses, to which she gave all the money subscribed to a testimonial for her: she was much interested in the reform of workhouses under the Poor Law, where the treatment of the sick was disgraceful. She well deserved the statue which commemorates her, side by side with Sidney Herbert, in Waterloo Place.

John Malcolm Ludlow (1821–1911), almost exactly Florence Nightingale's contemporary, was the real founder of the Christian Socialist Movement. He rejected Newman's view that the poor were only 'objects for compassion and benevolence' and agreed with Kingsley that religion was in danger of becoming 'an opium dose for keeping beasts of burden patient while they were being overloaded'. In the days of the

---

[1] When she was asked if she objected to Presbyterian nurses, she said that she did not care to what denomination they belonged, as long as they could nurse and did not weigh more than 14 stone, as the beds were not strong enough.

Chartists (1848) he issued, with the help of Maurice and Kingsley, a series of tracts called *Politics for the People* of which the leading principles were 'there will be no true freedom without virtue, no true science without religion, no true industry without the fear of God and love to your fellow-citizens.'

He organized a scheme of Working Associations on a co-operative basis, with the idea of ultimately transforming the whole system of industry, and when the Amalgamated Society of Engineers was founded in 1851 it adopted his principles, which had already been tried on a small scale in London.

Their scheme was wrecked by a lock-out, but Ludlow persevered. He succeeded in getting Co-operation legalized in 1852, but co-operative production is much more difficult to organize than co-operative distribution, and he came to the conclusion that more education was needed. The result was the founding of the Working Men's College in 1854, in which he was helped by F. D. Maurice and Tom Hughes: it still flourishes, though Ludlow left it when it seemed to place religion in a secondary place or allowed the religious motive to be taken for granted.

He had bridged the gulf between Christianity and Labour, and his work was carried on, though on less ambitious lines, by great men like Westcott, Scott Holland, and Gore: it is largely due to him that a really Christian democracy is a possible ideal for the English-speaking world, whereas elsewhere it is difficult for a Christian to be a socialist, a liberal, or a democrat.[1]

John Ruskin (1819–1900) and *William Morris* (1834–96) were so unmistakably inspired by Christianity in that passionate sympathy with the poor which made them turn from art to political economy that we need not inquire in what sense at different periods of their lives they would have claimed, or accepted, the Christian name. Both felt beauty to be a divine thing in which all men could and should share, and both felt society in their day to be 'ugly' in every sense of the word. On both these came 'with ever-increasing urgency the cry of

[1] *Christian Social Reformers of the Nineteenth Century* (edited Martin), pp. 147 ff.

a bewildered and unhappy people' (the words are from Morris), and both gave up their own ease and tastes and leisure to plead the cause of the poor. Though this cannot be said of *Charles Dickens* (1812–70), he not only accomplished much for social reform but had a very firm hold of the great Christian principle that 'there is no one too little or insignificant to belong to the great household of God.'[1]

Josephine Butler in 1869 after long searchings of heart felt it her duty to lead a campaign against laws which gave official sanction to the theory that there were and should be different standards of morality for men and women.

She was bitterly opposed and denounced in foul language in parliament, her meetings were broken up and her life often in danger. Her inspiration was entirely Christian: at one crisis of the campaign we find her writing; 'We read, we studied, we thought, we prayed as it were for our very lives.' She triumphed, as Wilberforce had triumphed, because she at last convinced the conscience of her fellow-countrymen. Her influence, like his, has extended far beyond the bounds of Great Britain, and she deserves the title once given her of a 'saint belonging to a world as wide as the world she pitied and helped'. Every Englishwoman should hold her name in honour.

The Co-operative Movement in this country has been unmistakably Christian in origin, and the Nonconformists in particular played a large and honourable part in its early days: it represented a very healthy, and a very Christian, reaction from the days when it was assumed that if every man cared only for himself in an intelligent way the result would be happiness for all. The same may, with more qualification, be said of the Trade Union Movement. It is at least a matter of history that many of those who played a large part in founding it were local preachers or teachers in their own Sunday schools, and the principles to which they appealed were definitely Christian principles, such as the equality of all men before God, and the right of every man to justice, and it may be recalled that *James Keir Hardie* (1856–1915), the first Labour

[1] *Christian Social Reformers of the Nineteenth Century* (edited Martin), p. 239.

member of Parliament (1892), a staunch member of the Evangelical Union, maintained always that 'Socialism is a great *moral* movement. I am a Socialist because Socialism means Fraternity founded on Justice': what this meant to him is made clear by the fact that towards the end of his life he said that were he to live it again, he would 'devote it to the advocacy of the Gospel of Christ.'[1]

The work done in hospitals (which, it should be remembered, were a Christian creation) is often to-day done by men and women who forget its Christian origin and would not accept the Christian creed: and the same is true of much splendid social work.

But it has always been part of the Christian creed that all goodness, all beauty and all truth have their source in God, and the wisest Christians have never been anxious to limit the meaning of the word inspiration. Just as

> Many a man for Christes sake
> Was martyred in Romayne[2]
> Ere any Christendom was knowe[3] there
> Or any cross honoured,

so work that is fundamentally Christian is being done now by countless people who do not 'profess and call themselves' His followers—but we have a right to claim that their work promotes His glory.

Here is a modern adaptation of part of the great eleventh chapter of the Epistle to the Hebrews which will illustrate this point of view:[4]

By faith William Wilberforce removed from England the guilt of the African slave-trade. By faith he, together with Thomas Clarkson, prepared the way for the abolition of slavery throughout the British Empire.

By faith Lord Shaftesbury gave up a life of peace and comfort to fight against apathy, prejudice, vested interests, and official obstruction that hapless folk should receive compassion and that mercy should prevail in the land; by faith he forced through Parliament the

---

[1] Martin, op. cit., p. 118.   [2] The Roman Empire.   [3] Known.
[4] It is taken with slight alterations and additions from *Life and Work, the Record of the Church of Scotland* (February 1941).

first Factory Act forbidding the employment of children under nine in factories; by faith he made illegal the employment of women and little children in coal pits; by faith he brought to an end the barbarous practice of sending boys and girls of four and five years of age up the inside of chimneys to sweep them.

By faith David Livingstone set sail for Africa, and sojourned in that strange country, not knowing whither he went; by faith he penetrated to the heart of the Dark Continent, bringing to light hidden iniquities and age-long cruelties; by faith he opened the way for the coming of the Gospel with healing and freedom in its wings.

By faith Florence Nightingale, when she was come to years, refused to be called the daughter of her wealthy father, choosing rather to suffer affliction in service to the neglected children of God than to enjoy the pleasures of London in the Season; by faith she led a band of trained nurses to care for the untended sick and wounded in the Crimea; by faith she overcame the obstacles of Army and Medical etiquette; by faith she passed through the Sea of Red Tape as by dry land, which the authorities essaying to hinder were put to confusion; by faith she created Sick-nursing as a ministry of enlightened skill, making science the hand-maid of mercy.

These all died in faith, not having received the promises, but having seen them afar off, and were persuaded of them, and embraced them, and confessed that they were but pioneers on the earth.

By faith William Booth and Catherine, his wife, endured ridicule, obloquy, and violence to carry the Gospel to the slums of Darkest England; by faith they brought Christian compassion to rescue the poorest and most forlorn.

By faith the founders of the Church Missionary Society set forth to repair the manifold wrongs done to Africa: by faith their missionaries went to India and China and Japan, not fearing the wrath of kings or princes, for they endured as seeing Him who is invisible; by faith they penetrated into Uganda and were not afraid of the king's commandment so that in very truth there sprang of one, and him as good as dead, as many as the stars of the sky in multitude and as the sand that is by the sea shore innumerable.

And what shall I more say? For time would fail me to tell of Richard Cobden and John Bright; of James Simpson and Lord Lister; of William Carey, Alexander Duff, and John Howard; of Mary Slessor also, Josephine Butler, and Elizabeth Fry; of Captain Scott, and Lawrence Oates (who being dead yet speaketh); and of all who through faith removed mountains, drained marshes, laid submarine cables, irrigated desert lands; who reformed prisons, changed the hell of lunatic asylums into a haven of mercy; found alleviation for pain; taught the blind to read; gave ears to the deaf; brought hope to the leper; who won for all children the chance of education; redressed ancient wrongs; achieved long-cherished hopes; cured incurable diseases, so that women received their dead restored to life again; others endured cruel sufferings; mockings, slanders, yea, moreover, bonds and imprisonment; some were killed while experimenting for the good of mankind, some lost fingers, arms, and life itself through working with deadly rays, dying that others might live; young men spent the best years of their lives in the trenches, amid rending steel and scorching flame and rats and lice and the stench of putrifying corpses; they were gassed; they were bayoneted; they were shot down from the sky on fire; they were drowned in the depths of the sea (of whom their world was not worthy); they campaigned in deserts and over mountains, and dwelt in dens and caves of the earth.

Wherefore, seeing we also are compassed about with this great cloud of witnesses to the power of faith, let us lay aside all that might hamper our running, and let us run with unswerving purpose the course that is set before us, looking unto Jesus, Who trod the path of faith before us and trod it to the end.

XXI

A DIALOGUE ON CHRISTIAN SOCIAL SERVICE

A CONVERSATION between two friends after a meeting of a Social Service Committee.

Clericus (*returning after seeing the members out*). Now we can have a cup of tea in peace! My word, how boring virtuous people can be and how they keep on talking!

Anticlericus. It's all very well for you to complain! they don't get the chance of holding forth every Sunday like you.

Clericus. Quite true—but I don't think any of our friends would fill the churches by their eloquence.

Anticlericus. You aren't as successful as all that yourself! I see they've started another discussion in the papers about why people don't go to church.

Clericus. Silly idiots!

Anticlericus (*laughing*). I thought you wouldn't like it: you can't find it very cheerful reading!

Clericus. Oh, it's not that—it's only that the subject seems to me so silly. The really interesting question is why people do things, not why they don't. There are any amount of strong reasons against doing anything that's worth doing. I should like to see a discussion as to why people *go* to church, not why they don't: I could answer the second question in my sleep.

Anticlericus. I'm sure I don't know why they go—I never go myself, and I can think of plenty of reasons——

Clericus (*interrupting*). Oh, I know—bad sermons, bad music, hard seats——

Anticlericus (*interrupting in his turn*). It's much more than that—it's because they've ceased to believe religion's any good.

Clericus. How did they find that out?

Anticlericus. They've read some history, for one thing, and they see what a lot of harm's been done in its name.

Clericus. Do you really think that's the fair test? A lot of harm's been done in the name of patriotism, or the British Empire, but I don't think that settles it: it seems to be fairer to ask what positive good either of them has done.

Anticlericus. Well, no one can say religion's doing much now: look at the last century, and all the good work that's been done in it—where does religion come in? Where are your great religious leaders?

Clericus. I quite agree there haven't been outstanding social reformers like Lord Shaftesbury—but there've been any amount of people who've followed him in a small way. After all, it was a Christian who started the reform of hospitals and the improvement of nursing, and the people who began the Trade Union Movement were very definitely Christians— quite a lot of the early leaders were local preachers.

Anticlericus. Nonconformists, most of them—not your lot at all!

Clericus. My dear man, my 'lot' as you call them, are the 'blessed company of all faithful people'—I don't grudge the Nonconformists or the Quakers all the credit they deserve— but still Charles Kingsley *was* a parson and Charles Gore *was* a bishop, and it would be silly to say that they didn't take an interest in the condition of the people!

Anticlericus. Yes, but all you religious people really think more about getting people to church than about improving the conditions under which they live.

Clericus. I don't think that's quite fair, either. Our job— what we're paid for, if you like to put it that way—is to see that people don't forget God: if they really remembered Him, our theory is that the other things would follow. It's very dangerous for religious people to get mixed up in politics.

Anticlericus. You've done that all right, whenever it suited you!

Clericus. Quite true, and we've always suffered for it! Whenever the Church, or the Nonconformists either for that matter, have become political, they've lost their real appeal. I don't think you can blame us for being nervous about that.

Anticlericus. As far as I can see, the main thing you religious people have done has been to squabble with one another about education—as if it really mattered just what brand of religion little children were taught!

Clericus. My dear Anticlericus, I've seldom heard so many fallacies and half-truths in one sentence! You might just as well say it didn't matter what kind of milk they drank: they've got a right to the best we can give them, and if we honestly think one brand of religion (as you call it) the best, we're bound to see they get it if possible. Not but what I agree that there's been a lot of silly and very un-Christian bitterness about it. The one thing that's clear is that a child has a right to be taught its parents' religion by some one who believes in it, and I'm thankful to say we've begun to see that at last.

And when you've said all the hard things you like about our quarrels, it's only fair to remember that it was Christian people who first began to take any interest in education at all, and spent any amount of money long before the State took a hand.

Anticlericus. Well, I hope you're getting a bit wiser now! Anyhow the solid fact is that any amount of the good work done in social things is done by people who aren't Christian at all.

Clericus. I shouldn't quite agree with that: I shouldn't say that a man 'isn't a Christian at all' if he behaved in a Christian way, whether he says the Christian creed or not.

Anticlericus. Oh, I see how you're going to try to get round it! You're going to say that all good work is really Christian, so that you have it both ways! Look at Romilly and Bentham, who first stirred people's consciences in the nineteenth century about the treatment of criminals. Both of them said they weren't Christian, but you calmly claim that they were.

Clericus. My dear man, it's not my job to decide if people are Christian or not, that's God's affair! I only say that if a man urges the sort of reforms Christ would wish to see I'm not going to be too much excited about his creed: of course I'm sorry he doesn't claim the name, but very likely it's because he met a very poor type of Christianity when he was young and never got over it.

All I say is that this country has a lot of latent or concealed Christianity in it, and that that's the only reason why it's doing what it is to-day. It was Christianity that first made justice and freedom and truth into virtues for the ordinary man, and that's soaked in somehow through the centuries.

Anticlericus. It's not fair, you know! You clergy get too much practice in talking! I'm not going to argue with you— but I'm not going to come and hear you preach, all the same!

Clericus. 'Nobody asked you, sir, she said!' But just answer one question. Why do people come to Committees like the one we've just been sitting on? What does it matter to them whether poor people get looked after or not? Why do you come yourself, if it comes to that?

Anticlericus. Well, any decent man with a conscience is bound to take some interest——

Clericus. And where did you get your standard of decency from? or who told you either that you'd got a conscience, or that you ought to obey it? I think I know: you think you don't—that's really the difference between us.

Anticlericus. Now, now, I came here for a peaceful committee, and you're trying to let me in for a sermon! I must be going home. I'm much obliged for your tea, especially in these days, but even tea can be bought too dear! It'll take more than your arguments to persuade me to be a Christian.

Clericus (*helping him on with his coat*). You remind me of the chap in Molière who found he'd been talking prose all his life and had never known it.

Anticlericus (*laughing*). So you really think I'm good enough to come to church?

Clericus. My good man, people don't come to church because they're good!

Anticlericus. Why *do* they come? We're back where we started!

Clericus. Because they think they ought to be better—that's the reason why there are so precious few of them. Good night!

XXII

A CENTURY OF GROWTH IN CHRISTIAN UNITY

THE Oxford Movement profoundly affected religious life throughout England: every parish church, and most Nonconformist chapels, have felt its influence, sometimes in the way in which ministers are robed (it is hard to remember that the surplice was once thought a popish vestment), and always in the music and the hymns. It is interesting to notice how, in any popular hymn book, the names of Christians of every type stand side by side, Roman Catholic and Methodist, Anglican and Calvinist, mystic, revivalist, layman, ecclesiastic, sinner, and saint.

The High Church Movement to which it gave birth has revived many practices once wrongly thought to be identified with Rome: since the war of 1914–18 it has seemed natural to hear prayers for the dead in churches or chapels which could not be suspected of Roman leanings. Ritual has developed in some Congregationalist gatherings as well as in Anglican churches: it may not always be dignified and may sometimes be fussy, but at least it is realized that those who find care for external things to be a help to their religion need not therefore be accused of superstition.

There are two attitudes of mind which are equally legitimate: some may say that the worship of God calls for everything which can be done to make it worthy of Him and that beauty of all kinds should be used in its service: others hold that everything of the kind only serves to distract the attention from the one purpose of all worship, which is intercourse with God. Those who are responsible for the organizing of Christian services should seek, in the wise words of the preface on ceremonies in the Prayer Book, 'not so much to please and satisfy either of these parties as how to please God and profit them both.'

Ritual may no doubt suggest doctrines which the Reformation definitely put aside, but this is not the place to discuss such questions, which concern only the internal discipline of the Church of England. There are some who are shocked at the differences allowed to exist between one Anglican church and another, but others regard it as a glory of the Church of England that it does not aim at a rigid uniformity but allows scope for different temperaments. The book of Common Prayer provides an elastic standard. It has always aimed at keeping that middle course which was laid down by its great doctors in the seventeenth century.

The various Nonconformist bodies have their own problems and their own ways of enforcing discipline: they, like the Church of England, have in the last century been readier to admit honest differences of opinion and practice, where fundamental doctrines are not concerned. Nothing is more remarkable in the religious history of the last hundred years than the growth of religious scholarship, and here Christians of all kinds have been able to work together, not by any means always agreeing, but with a real respect for learning wherever it has been shown.

This has been particularly clear in the matter of biblical criticism. A hundred years ago very few Christians doubted the almost verbal inspiration of the Bible and the first teachers of evolution were passionately denounced. To-day all Christian scholars are agreed that the Bible should be regarded rather as a library than as a single book, and that its primary purpose is not to teach science or history but the gradual revelation of the truth about God and His dealings with man.

In bringing about this change Anglicans and Nonconformists have worked side by side and neither claims any monopoly of learning in any part of the field, and both rely on the other's results.[1] This is an inestimable gain, and has led to a mutual respect: the atmosphere has changed, and not only in the mission field but also at home their leaders have been able to discuss their differences with a sympathy and a desire to find agreement which has never existed since Nonconformity first began. As has been said, it really seems that agreement may soon be reached in the deplorable dispute about religious education and there is at least a hope of wider agreement still. It looks as if Christians were beginning seriously to consider what is implied in Christ's words, 'By this shall all men know that ye are my disciples, if ye have love one to another.'

Not long ago at a conference at Lausanne, attended by representatives of all Christian bodies except the Roman Catholics and the Baptists, it was agreed that the essentials of a true Church were: (1) the Scriptures, (2) the two Creeds (the Apostles' and the Nicene), (3) the two Sacraments of the Gospel, (4) a ministry universally recognized.[2] This is at least a position infinitely more hopeful than could have been dreamt of a century ago.

It is the obvious duty of all Christians to do anything they can to help on the reunion of Christendom: every one can at least try to understand his neighbour's point of view. He may find that the points which divide them are neither so numerous nor so vital as he supposed. What does it mean to be a Christian?

For example, it was Dr. Drummond, a Unitarian, who gave perhaps the best argument that it was in fact St. John who wrote the Gospel which bears his name.

[2] The position of the Quakers causes a difficulty. They reject much which all other Christians think essential, but their practical Christianity is so obvious that they may perhaps be classed as honorary members of any Christian Church. The Quaker achievement at Bournville should be mentioned as a notable contribution towards solving the problems of housing and factory management.

EPILOGUE

WE have been trying to see how Christianity came to this country, and what its influence there has been and is. The first part of the task is easy: the second is difficult for two reasons.

In the first place no Christian can feel that its effect has been nearly as great as it ought to have been, and the more he believes in his religion the readier he will be to admit its failures. The result may well be that in any history they show up much more clearly than anything else, and that the reader may come to feel that Christians have been more occupied in disputes about comparatively small things than in those which really matter. We have to remember that all through the centuries there have been countless places in which men and women whose names never get into the history books have been taught, and have been trying, to follow Christ, and that they are the people who have made the national character. In old days they were found perhaps mainly in the monas-teries; now they form the faithful congregations of innumer-able parish churches and chapels: in old days their unity may have been clearer than it is to-day, but then and now they are united by the faith which Christ taught and in the attempt to live as He would wish.

It is silly to blame Christianity for the bad behaviour of some who call themselves Christians but make no effort to live up to their belief, just as it would be silly to blame a medicine for doing no good when it was never taken, but kept on the shelf. We have no means of deciding who has a right to the name: to attempt to keep out those who 'are not good enough' would involve inquiries which we have no right to make—and so Christianity gets a blame which it does not deserve. If you want to know what cricket or football really is, you go to the grounds where they are played by experts, and if you want to know what Christianity is you must study the men and women who are really trying to live by it. You will have seen some examples of such people in this book, but you must never forget the unknown millions to whom

Christianity has given a purpose and a hope in life, and who have played so great a part in making England a better and a happier country.

Our second difficulty is (as was said in the last chapter) that the Christian influence shows itself in the lives of very many people who, for different reasons, would not call themselves Christians. That has become very clear in these last years. We are fighting for great causes such as justice between man and man, freedom to think and worship as you wish, and truth and honour between nations. These seem to us all to be of first-rate importance and we are all ready to suffer for their sake, and proud that our country is called upon to do so.

But we often forget that it is belief in the Christian God which has fixed these ideas, or ideals, in our hearts. No one would suggest that the Christian Church has always been true to any of them, but no one can deny that it was the Christian teaching which, as a matter of history, made Englishmen believe that every man, because he is the child of God, has a right to fair dealing, and to liberty, and an obligation to tell the truth. Whenever Christians have forgotten any of these things we know that they were being false to their Master's teaching. It is very unfortunate that popes and cardinals, bishops and priests, and 'respectable' Christians of all sorts should have been such poor representatives of their faith, but it does not really matter. The one thing which *does* matter is whether Christ's teaching about God and man is true, and what that teaching was the New Testament will tell us.

The English character has been built up on that foundation, and it can hardly be an accident that our enemies have increasingly rejected it, for it is a definitely un-Christian thing to treat man as having no right to freedom or to justice. If we were to give up our faith, there is no security that we should not go the same way, for it is very hard to go on believing in man unless you believe in the God Who made him, and made him for a purpose.

You cannot live a life without some faith behind it, any more than you can really play a game without some knowledge of its theory. It is the Christian faith, or theory, slowly worked out and slowly applied, which has brought about all the changes for the better in the life of this country. There are many more that are still needed, but the spirit which inspires them and the power which carries them out will both be found in the Gospel of Christ. In so far as this book is a story of failure, as it largely is, it is full of encouragement, for the moral is that whenever Christians have failed it has been because they forgot their faith, and whenever they were true to it they have succeeded.

> I give you the end of a golden string;
>   Only wind it into a ball,
> It will lead you in at Heaven's gate,
>   Built in Jerusalem's wall.

INDEX